Beating Your Eating Disorder: A Cognitive-Behavioral Self-Help Guide for Adult Sufferers and their Carers

Beating Your Eating Disorder: A Cognitive-Behavioral Self-Help Guide for Adult Sufferers and their Carers

Glenn Waller

Consultant Clinical Psychologist, Vincent Square Eating Disorders Service,
Central and North West London NHS Foundation Trust, and Eating Disorders Section,
Institute of Psychiatry, King's College London, UK.

Victoria Mountford

Principal Clinical Psychologist, Eating Disorders Service, South London and
Maudsley NHS Foundation Trust, London, UK, and Honorary Research Fellow,
Institute of Psychiatry, King's College London, UK.

Rachel Lawson

Senior Clinical Psychologist, South Island Eating Disorders, Canterbury District Health
Board, and the Anxiety Clinic, Christchurch, New Zealand.

Emma Gray (née Corstorphine)

Consultant Clinical Psychologist/Service Coordinator, The British CBT & Counselling Service,
and Fellow at the Institute of Psychiatry, King's College London, UK.

Helen Cordery

Trainee psychotherapist at the John Bowlby Centre, London, UK, and former specialist
registered dietitian working with eating disorders.

Hendrik Hinrichsen

Consultant Clinical Psychologist and Clinical Lead, Sutton & Merton IAPT,
South West London & St. George's NHS Trust, and Visiting Research Fellow,
Institute of Psychiatry, King's College London, UK.

CAMBRIDGE
UNIVERSITY PRESS

CAMBRIDGE UNIVERSITY PRESS
Cambridge, New York, Melbourne, Madrid, Cape Town, Singapore,
São Paulo, Delhi, Dubai, Tokyo, Mexico City

Cambridge University Press
The Edinburgh Building, Cambridge CB2 8RU, UK

Published in the United States of America by Cambridge University Press, New York

www.cambridge.org
Information on this title: www.cambridge.org/9780521739047

First published 2010

Printed in the United Kingdom at the University Press, Cambridge

A catalog record for this publication is available from the British Library

Library of Congress Cataloging-in-Publication data

Beating your eating disorder : a cognitive-behavioral self-help guide for adult
sufferers and their carers / Glenn Waller ... [et al.].
    p.   cm.
  ISBN 978-0-521-73904-7 (pbk.)
  1. Eating disorders–Treatment–Popular works.   2. Cognitive therapy–Popular works.
I. Waller, Glenn.   II. Title.
  RC552.E18B44 2011
  616.85′26–dc22

                                                           2010017814

ISBN 978-0-521-73904-7 Paperback

Praise for *Beating Your Eating Disorder*

"Decades of clinical experience come to light in this plain-speaking self-help text for both sufferers and carers. There's no sugar-coating here, just a pragmatic and evidence-informed step-by-step approach for gaining control of your own eating disorder. Through the use of rich vignettes and colorful analogies, the authors provide a context for recovery. The chapter on motivation is a unique contribution that allows both sufferers and carers to self-appraise their readiness for change. The book is infused with hope for recovery provided the reader is prepared to dig-in and do the work necessary for a successful self-help journey."

Cindy Bulik, William Jeanne Jordan Distinguished Professor of Eating Disorders, University of North Carolina at Chapel Hill, USA.

"Comprehensive and thorough. The information is provided in an approachable and forthright style. The authors clearly describe what is involved in overcoming an eating disorder and encourage the reader to do the necessary work.

It doesn't underestimate the effort it will take, but rather gives very helpful, practical and evidence based information. The book is equally helpful for families and friends of someone working to beat their eating disorder – giving them the support they need to be a powerful ally in recovery. Most importantly, this book gives hope that life without an eating disorder can be lived to the full."

Susan Ringwood, Chief Executive, beat, UK nationwide self-help organization for sufferers of eating disorders.

"This clearly written self-help guide for adults with eating disorders successfully translates the best available treatment we have – cognitive behavioral therapy – into a user-friendly and highly practical self-help approach. It is thorough and detailed without being overly long, and the material is presented in a fresh, interesting way. This excellent book is highly recommended for adult sufferers with eating disorders who wish to use a self-help guide for the first step, and hopefully the only step that will be necessary, in overcoming their eating problems."

James Mitchell, Christoferson Professor and Chair, Department of Clinical Neuroscience and Chester Fritz Distinguished University Professor, University of North Dakota School of Medicine and Health Sciences, USA.

"The writers communicate in a clear, direct, compassionate and honest voice, enriched by extensive clinical experience, that will help the reader to feel understood, to understand what maintains their eating disorder, and to have the courage to experiment with learning to eat healthily again.

This is a valuable resource for people with eating disorders considering change, for carers who feel lost, and for therapists who are seeking to help their clients build a foundation for enduring change."

Tracey Wade, Professor of Psychology, Flinders University, Australia.

"This is the long-overdue book that adult sufferers of an eating disorder and their carers have been waiting for. It has been masterfully written from a wealth of practical experience and will without doubt become a mandatory resource. It surpasses any of the other self-help guides in quality and scope, and will ensure that those who read it are impelled to act."

Stephen Touyz, Professor of Psychology, The University of Sydney, Australia.

Contents

Preface: read this bit first

Who is this book for?

If you are an adult who suffers from an eating disorder, this book is designed to help you overcome your eating problems. It is designed to help you regain control whether you have anorexia nervosa, bulimia nervosa, or an atypical problem (where you have some of the symptoms but do not meet all the criteria for one of those better-known diagnoses). You might have been directed to this book by a clinician (e.g., your family doctor might have recommended it, or a specialist clinician might have suggested that you try it while you wait for more formal treatment). However, many sufferers will never have received a formal diagnosis, but will know that they are not happy with their eating and their associated thoughts and feelings. This book is for you, whether or not you have a diagnosis.

If you are a carer, relative, partner, friend or child of a sufferer, this book is designed to help you advise, support, and work with the sufferer as she or he works to overcome the eating problem. This process includes learning how to cope with your own level of stress and concern, because you are likely to be severely affected by the sufferer's experiences. If you can deal with your own feelings, then you are in a stronger position to support the sufferer.

Our aim is to help any adult sufferer to eat normally again, without being plagued by worries about their shape or weight, and without feeling that you are out of control. If that is too much to imagine, then we aim to help you get as far along that path as you are ready to go right now. This book is not aimed at adolescents with eating problems, because the evidence is that such sufferers benefit more from a family-oriented approach. However, there are lessons in here that might be useful ones to add to the family perspective.

This book will *not* be enough for you if you have serious complications from your eating disorder. For example, we strongly recommend that you should seek professional support from your doctor if:
- you are very depressed or feel hopeless all the time
- you have physical symptoms of your eating problem that place you in danger (see the start of Section 1 on staying safe)
- you are using self-damaging behaviors (e.g., self-cutting, binge-drinking)
- you have a young child who you fear might be suffering as a result of your eating problems

You might still be able to use this book, but only when those other issues are dealt with and you are safe and stable.

You might be afraid that going to your doctor will be difficult or embarrassing, but if you go to your doctor with a clear idea of your concerns then she or he has a much better chance of helping you. You will not be the first sufferer or carer that your doctor has seen and there are very clear guidelines that your doctor can use to help in your care and support. One such recommendation is that many sufferers should be encouraged to try a self-help book ahead of any referral to specialist services. A good example is the National Institute for Health and Clinical Excellence (NICE) guideline on eating disorders for professionals, which is available online at: http://guidance.nice.org.uk/CG9/niceguidance/pdf/. There is a linked version of this document for sufferers and carers, which we recommend that you read. This version is available online at: http://guidance.nice.org. uk/CG9/publicinfo/pdf/.

What is this book about?

The self-help approach outlined here is based on the strongest evidence-based approach that currently exists for working with adults with eating disorders – cognitive behavioral therapy, also known as CBT. This form of therapy is not an easy solution to your problems, but it has been proven to have the strongest and/or fastest impact on most types of eating disorder (other than anorexia nervosa) among adults, and is more effective than most other forms of therapy for these disorders. Recent evidence also supports this approach with anorexia nervosa, although the evidence base is not as large.

Final points before starting

It is important that you remember that there are no miracle cures for eating disorders. If there were then it is pretty likely that you would already have found one that worked for you. Doing CBT is not easy – it is hard work. You can probably bet that the harder you work at it, the more likely this approach is to work for you.

So remember, simply owning this book is not the same as using it. Too many of our patients have bought books like this and then waited for them to be helpful, rather than putting them into action. You would be better not to buy this book (or any other) than simply have it sitting on a shelf. For this book to help you, you need to read it and use it. Using this book means learning how to do CBT and applying it to yourself – to take on the role of being your own therapist. There are many tasks in this book that you will find hard, but remember that the reward is that you get to eat normally again and to lead a life where every thought, feeling, and decision is not influenced by what you eat, your shape and your weight.

If your eating disorder were an easy problem to solve, you would have solved it already. Eating disorders are real, serious and complex problems. That complexity makes them difficult to resolve, but with the right approach it is possible to overcome them.

So a key thing to remember is that overcoming your eating disorder is going to be a complex and challenging task, and that it will require you learning to eat healthily again in order to succeed. That will mean working to develop an appropriate structure to your eating, and then changing the content of what you eat. Your thoughts, feelings, relationships, and motivation will all be important, but working on them without working on your eating (from the beginning) is unlikely to help you to escape your eating disorder.

Who are the authors of this book?

We are clinicians with many years of experience in working with the whole range of eating disorders, using CBT to help people with eating disorders to eat healthily and to feel good about themselves. Our goal in writing this book is to make this approach available to many sufferers (and their carers) who find it difficult to get clinical help, for whatever reason.

Acknowledgements

We would like to thank the many colleagues, trainees, and patients who have helped us to shape our ideas and the program that we have outlined here. We would also like to thank all of the editorial and production teams at Cambridge University Press for their encouragement, patience and assistance throughout the preparation of this book. Although others have played a valuable role, particular thanks are due to Richard Marley, Katie James and Frances Peck.

We would like to dedicate this book to our families.

About the authors

Glenn Waller has worked in the field of eating disorders for over 20 years. He works as a Consultant Clinical Psychologist for the Vincent Square Eating Disorders Service, Central and North West London NHS Foundation Trust, where his clinical specialty is cognitive behavioral therapy for eating disorders. He is also Visiting Professor of Psychology at the Institute of Psychiatry, King's College London. He has published over 200 peer-reviewed papers and 20 book chapters on the pathology and treatment of eating disorders, and has presented his work at many national and international conferences. He is also the lead author of a book on cognitive behavioral therapy for eating disorders (Waller, G., Cordery, H., Corstorphine, E., *et al.* [2007]). He is a member of the international Eating Disorders Research Society and the British Association for Behavioural and Cognitive Psychotherapies, and is a Fellow of the Academy for Eating Disorders. He is registered as a practitioner with the Health Professions Council.

Victoria Mountford is a Principal Clinical Psychologist with the Eating Disorders Service, South London and Maudsley NHS Foundation Trust and an Honorary Research Fellow at the Institute of Psychiatry, King's College London. She has both published and presented widely on eating disorders and has a particular interest in body image in eating disorders. She is currently involved in large treatment trials to evaluate the use of psychological therapies, including CBT, in anorexia nervosa. She is also co-author of a book on cognitive behavioral therapy for eating disorders (Waller, G., Cordery, H., Corstorphine, E., *et al.* [2007]). Victoria is an accredited member of the British Association of Behavioural and Cognitive Psychotherapy and the British Psychological Society, and is a registered practitioner with the Health Professions Council.

Rachel Lawson is a Senior Clinical Psychologist at the South Island Eating Disorders, Canterbury District Health Board in New Zealand, and is in private practice with the Anxiety Clinic, Christchurch, New Zealand. She has published research on eating disorders and regularly teaches about this area. She presents at national and international conferences on eating disorders.

Emma Gray (née Corstorphine) was Consultant Clinical Psychologist/Clinical Manager with the Oxford and Buckinghamshire Eating Disorders Service until recently. She left this post to expand her private practice (The British CBT & Counselling Service) and her family. She has published peer-reviewed papers and a book chapter on eating disorders and has presented papers and workshops at national and international conferences. She is also co-author of a book on cognitive behavioural therapy for eating disorders (Waller, G., Cordery, H., Corstorphine, E., *et al.* [2007]). She is a member of The British Psychological Society and the British Association for Behavioural and Cognitive Psychotherapies. She is registered with the Health Professions Council. She is a Visiting Research Fellow at the Institute of Psychiatry, King's College London.

Helen Cordery had been a dietitian for about 17 years at the time of co-writing this book, 12 of which had been spent specializing in working with people with eating disorders. This work was mainly within the National Health Service (NHS) and within a variety of settings (with outpatients, and on both in-patient and day-patient units). She is currently in the process of training to become an attachment-based psychotherapist.

Hendrik Hinrichsen is a Consultant Clinical Psychologist and Clinical Lead for the Sutton & Merton IAPT Service based in Wimbledon, London. He is also a Visiting Research Fellow at the Institute of Psychiatry, King's College London. Dr Hinrichsen has both published and presented research on cognitive behavioral therapy (CBT) for eating disorders and anxiety disorders, and he is the co-author of a book on CBT for eating disorders (Waller, G., Cordery, H., Corstorphine, E., *et al.* [2007]). In 2003 and 2009, he was a joint recipient of South West London Excellence Awards for clinically relevant research and working in partnership. Dr Hinrichsen is registered as a professional psychologist with the Health Professions Council, and he is fully accredited by the British Association for Behavioural and Cognitive Psychotherapies (BABCP).

Getting started

This section contains important information that will help you decide how to use the rest of the book. We use the section to outline:
- who this book is for, and why cognitive behavioral therapy (CBT) is likely to be relevant to you
- the key elements of CBT for the eating disorders
- how to read this book to get the maximum benefit

First things first: staying physically safe and well enough to use the help provided in this book

However, before you go any further with this approach, it is vital that you make sure that you (or the sufferer) are physically safe. Self-help can help you with many aspects of an eating problem, but there are some problems that require additional help. The eating disorders have a physical and emotional/psychological component, and both need to be addressed. Therefore, you should discuss the physical symptoms with your family physician anyway. However, if you (or the sufferer) experience any of the following, then you must get extra support and monitoring from your doctor in order to ensure safety:
- losing weight rapidly over several weeks (e.g., more than 1kg a week for more than four weeks)
- fainting, dizziness or blackouts
- your BMI (body mass index) is less than 16 (we will show you how to work out your BMI shortly)
- vomiting (especially if it is happening more than twice a day and/or you see blood in the vomit)
- taking laxatives frequently
- taking diet pills
- muscular weakness (e.g., you cannot stand without using your arms to lever yourself up)

- shortness of breath
- suffering from other medical conditions that affect your diet (e.g., diabetes, cystic fibrosis), as well as your eating problem
- binge drinking of alcohol
- self-harm (e.g., self-cutting or burning)
- feelings of hopelessness or suicidal thoughts

Listing these points might sound like we are trying to scare you, but part of working on your eating disorder is reducing the risks of these very real and dangerous physical symptoms. As the signs and symptoms above can place you at risk of serious physical consequences (e.g., heart irregularities, electrolyte imbalance), the first step in managing and resolving your eating disorder must be to ensure your physical safety. Therefore, it is important to get yourself checked out. Your doctor might simply assess the risk (e.g., doing some blood tests, testing your heart function) and give you the "all clear", but she or he might want to offer you some help with these problems (e.g., potassium supplements). She or he might also suggest that you should be referred for specialist help with your eating or other problems. (*It is important to remember that comparatively few individuals with an eating disorder are ever admitted to hospital, so being referred for such specialist help does not mean that you are going to need to be admitted.*) However, as recommended in the NICE guidelines for eating problems (see the Preface), many doctors will suggest that you should try a self-help approach, even while waiting for that support. That brings you back to this book.

Who is this book for?

This book is for you whether you have an eating disorder or whether you are a carer for someone who suffers from an eating disorder (e.g., a partner, a parent or a best friend). Ideally, both the sufferer and her or his carer will read it, and share their thoughts. If you are the one who has the eating problems, then this book is for you, whether you are male or female, whatever your age, whatever your ethnicity, and whatever the nature of your eating disorder.[1] We think that every sufferer needs to learn how to be her or his own CBT therapist, but all this effort can be made much more effective if she or he has the support of someone close who understands the problem and who knows what CBT involves. As putting CBT into practice can be challenging, having someone close to coach you during this process can be invaluable and can sometimes make the difference between failure and success.

Here are some questions to ask yourself at this point:

Question one: "Do I have an eating disorder?"

First and foremost, this book is likely to be for you if you believe that you have issues about your eating and about your body. You might feel that those issues are getting in the way of living your life in the way you want. Sufferers of eating disorders often have concerns about their eating, shape and weight, and they report high levels of anxiety about what would happen if they ate normally (i.e., like other people around them). The result is that you use eating-related behaviors to cope with your beliefs and fears – maybe food restriction, maybe exercise, maybe taking laxatives, diuretic or diet pills, maybe overeating or binge-eating.

---

[1] Please note that this book is not for individuals who are simply overweight. However, it will be entirely relevant to someone who is overweight and who also binge-eats, for example.

Table 1.1 Questionnaire 1a: Do I have a problem with my eating?

Just tick the answer that most closely describes your feelings or actions on each of these points:	Not at all	A little	Sometimes	Most of the time	All of the time
I spend time worrying about whether I have put on weight					
I worry that my body will get bigger if I don't keep my eating very tightly controlled					
I have to restrict what I eat and/or exercise in order to compensate for the fact that I have eaten too much					
I take laxatives and/or make myself sick to help control my weight and size					
My eating pattern means that I cannot live the life that I want to					
I spend a lot of time checking my weight, measuring myself, checking my reflection, etc.					
I feel ashamed of my eating pattern					
My eating distresses those around me (my family, friends, etc.)					
My health suffers as a result of my eating					
My relationships are limited because I have an eating problem					
I eat because I am upset, rather than because I am hungry					
Controlling what I eat is more important than any other element of my life					
I exercise a lot, even if I am injured or it gets in the way of socializing with my friends (professional athletes excepted)					

You are also likely to find that eating, and weight and shape concerns have a big influence over how you organize your life. Although this way of coping might have given you a sense of control at first, it is likely to have ended up creating more problems than it solved initially. Tick off your answers in the questionnaire above (Table 1.1).

The more that your answers appear in the columns on the right hand side, the worse your problem is right now. We will come back to these questions later in the book to see if your attitudes, feelings and behaviors change as you work on your treatment.

You will notice that there is nothing in the questionnaire about your age, gender, ethnicity, or type of eating disorder (e.g., anorexia nervosa or bulimia nervosa).

This is because the stereotype of an eating disorder sufferer (young, female, white, and anorexic) is misleading. Although eating disorders are more likely to be found among younger females, anyone can develop an eating disorder.

Question two: "Does my eating problem really deserve any attention?"

One of the most common themes when sufferers come to a specialist center for the treatment of their eating problem is: "I don't deserve any help – other people need it more." They are almost always wrong. If you are concerned about your eating and body shape, and if it is impairing your life, then your eating disorder deserves attention and this book is for you.

While every eating disorder manifests differently, it is useful to think about some general profiles that might give you an idea of whether your eating problems are comparable and need attention. These three cases are all females, but they could equally be males. We will come back to these cases as the book progresses, to illustrate how you can use this approach to help yourself move on from your eating disorder. Please remember that there is not enough space here to describe every individual who develops an eating disorder, but many of the themes in these cases should be familiar, particularly:

- the sufferer's extreme concern about eating, weight and shape
- the behaviors that follow those beliefs and that maintain them
- the way that the eating attitudes and behaviors significantly impair the life of the sufferer and carers

---

Case 1: Jenny

Jenny is a 32-year-old woman who has had anorexia for over 14 years. She developed her problem at a time of considerable stress, when her parents were divorcing in the run-up to her school examinations. In order to get a sense of control over some aspect of her life, she began to diet. Initially, this led her to feel a positive "buzz" as she lost weight. However, that was followed by feeling scared of weight gain and having to diet even harder. While her weight is low, she has only ever been hospitalized once, when she was 19. Since then, she has maintained her weight near the top of the anorexic weight range. This has allowed her to work, but she feels that she has not reached her potential in her profession. Nor has she been able to sustain a relationship. Almost all of her free time is taken up with exercising in her local gym, trying to deal with how fat she feels. Although she would like to have children, she is not biologically able to do so at present, because her low

Case 1: (cont.)

weight means that her ovaries have become non-functional and her periods have stopped. In addition, she had a bone scan two years ago that indicated substantial osteoporosis (loss of bone structure). Jenny's mood is low and her concentration is poor. She has investigated getting help twice, but still feels afraid of engaging in such change.

Case 2: Katy

Katy, aged 23, has bulimia nervosa. She is slightly above the normal weight range, at least partly because of the binge-eating, which she does four or five times per week. She tries to control her weight by missing meals and snacks and by exercising, but when she binges she makes herself vomit so that she can reduce her anxiety about gaining weight. She weighs herself up to 20 times per day, to feel safe about her weight being stable. Sometimes, she takes laxatives to try to compensate for the larger binges. She describes all her thoughts as being about how others see her and about whether they see her as fat. She occasionally cuts herself when she feels very distressed, in order to cope with those difficult feelings. At other times, she drinks to cope with her fear that others will be judging her negatively.

Case 3: Polly

Polly is 44 and works as a teacher. She has a substantial record of absence from work for reasons of illness. Like very many people with an eating disorder, she does not fit neatly into an "anorexia" or "bulimia" category. She has been concerned about her eating, weight and shape for all of her adult life. She is also very concerned with eating "healthily," which means that she eats from a limited range of foods (most of which are low in fat and carbohydrate). The result is that her overall diet is poor and unbalanced. She is slightly underweight, but is not losing weight and is not in the anorexic weight range. She reports that she binges, but this is actually her way of describing eating any foods that she had not planned to eat. She vomits when she has eaten in that way. She has children and her partner is concerned that they are developing similar concerns about eating, weight and shape (though Polly herself does not accept that this is necessarily true or a worry). She is more concerned that her eating pattern is the reason that she has been passed over for promotion. Following a visit to a diet clinic and a set of unverified "tests," she reports a range of food intolerances and irritable bowel syndrome (although full medical investigations have failed to confirm these self-diagnoses).

Question three: "What can I do if I care for or live with someone with an eating disorder?"

This book is also for you if you are a carer for someone with an eating problem. Maybe you are a parent, partner or other family member, and you are concerned that your child, partner, sister, brother or relative has a problem. Alternatively, maybe you are worried about a friend's eating and want to know how to help them. Living with someone with an eating disorder can be challenging and exhausting, so there may be some real value in being able to understand what challenges they will have to overcome in order to get better and in being able to assist them in this process. The next set of questions (Table 1.2) is for you as a

Table 1.2 Questionnaire 2a: Does my relative/child/partner/parent/friend have an eating problem, and how is it affecting her/his life and mine?

Just tick the answer that most closely describes your feelings on each of these points. Because this questionnaire is for all types of sufferer, we have not specified who the sufferer is (e.g., your child, your partner, your friend, or your parent):	Not at all	A little	Sometimes	Most of the time	All of the time
The sufferer's eating controls her/his life					
The sufferer feels that she/he is in control of eating, but that is not the case					
My relationship with the sufferer is poorer because of her/his eating pattern					
My relationship with the sufferer is stressful because of issues around food and eating					
My life is constrained by the sufferer's eating and body concerns and related behaviors					
I wish that I could have a normal relationship with the sufferer, untainted by food					
Our whole relationship is influenced by the sufferer's eating					
I can see that the sufferer's quality of life is really suffering, and she or he is not developing as she/he could					
The sufferer's eating takes up so much of her or his time, that she/he has no time for a happy life					
I am stressed by the sufferer's eating problems and how they affect her/his behavior					
My own eating suffers as a result of the sufferer's rules and behaviors about food					
My other relationships are damaged by the sufferer's eating problems					

carer, asking you to think about whether the individual has a problem, and whether that problem is distressing for you. Again, we will come back to these questions later in the book, to see if things have changed.

As with the questionnaire for the sufferer (above), the more that your answers appear in the boxes on the right hand side, the stronger are your concerns for the sufferer and the more their eating difficulties are affecting your life right now. We will come back to these questions later in the book to see how things have changed as you gather the support and knowledge that will put you in a stronger position to help the sufferer.

If you and the sufferer have both completed your questionnaires, then now would be a good time to share your perspectives. Try reading one another's answers and discussing your viewpoints, but make sure you do that at a calm time, well away from food and meals and not when either of you is angry or upset.

Question four: "Why should I use self-help, rather than getting more formal help from a professional now?"

It is difficult to say which treatment method is best and for whom. Sufferers and carers need to find what is right for them, and this may change over time. For many people, self-help methods are enough to help them, but many others ultimately decide to seek out professional help. You may find that this book can also help you if:

- you are not yet ready to take the next step towards seeking professional help (e.g., too busy to attend when a clinic can see you; or feeling too ashamed and fearful of discussing your concerns with someone you don't know), and self-help is an alternative to seeking more formal help
- you find it hard to access appropriate specialist help (e.g., financial reasons, unavailability of effective treatment, time on a waiting list, geographical location)
- you need help to prepare for entering more formal treatment at a later stage.
In this book, we will tell you what to look for in formal treatment, and why You might also appreciate the support that you could get from talking to fellow sufferers and carers. In such cases we recommend that you should get in touch with a local support network (please see Appendix 1 for a list of such support organizations).

Question five: "So what do I do now?"

In this book, we want to share with you the information and strategies that we have found helpful in our work with patients over the years. Before we describe the details of our approach, here is a brief outline of what we think are the key elements of good treatment. First, you will learn about CBT and self-help. This is background information, giving you a context to understand what to do and why we will be asking you to do it. Therefore, we think this section should be essential reading for sufferers and carers alike. Next, we describe how to use the book. We hope that at this point you will feel ready to put at least some of what you have read into action and start to work on the eating problem – either as a sufferer or as a carer.

The key elements of cognitive behavioral therapy and the self-help approach

What is cognitive behavioral therapy (CBT)?

This chapter will help you to understand CBT – the most effective psychological treatment for most people with eating disorders. It is addressed to the sufferer, but it is relevant to carers too, so everyone should read it. The clearer your understanding, the better your position will be to make a decision about change, to make changes, or to support someone else to make changes. A shared understanding with those around you will make the path to recovery an easier one.

The key elements of CBT

CBT is a treatment approach that provides us with a way of understanding our experience of the world, enabling us to make changes if we need to. It does this by dividing our experience into four central components: thoughts (cognitions), feelings (emotions), behaviors and physiology (your biology). The CBT approach suggests that if you can learn to identify and understand these four elements and how they interact, you will be able to explain your problems and how to solve them. These four elements are linked together in Figure 2.1 (known as the "hot cross bun"), showing that all four influence each other. This structure means that we have to work on all four to create lasting change.

The CBT model does not ignore other factors that are relevant to eating disorders (e.g., environmental triggers, motivation, social settings, relationships). Rather, CBT focuses on the four key elements as being the target of therapy, but sees these other factors as potentially needing to be addressed in order to be able to focus on the physiology, behaviors, cognitions and emotions.

Very often, people who have had psychological help for their eating problems have been encouraged to change only some aspects of their experience (e.g., addressing their thoughts and emotions in isolation; or simply eating more), but not others. However, because of the interlinked nature of these aspects,

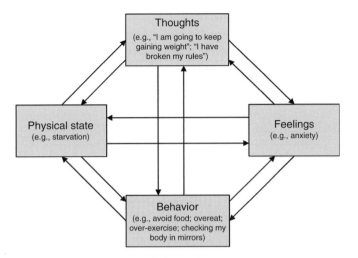

Fig. 2.1 The CBT "hot cross bun," showing the links between thoughts, feelings, physical state and behaviors.

changing only one or two is not sufficient to facilitate long-term change. The CBT model needs to address all the four core components of our experience – thoughts, feelings, behavior and physiology – to ensure that changes are robust and enduring.

For example, Katy (see earlier) had previously sought help on two occasions. On the first, the recommendation was simply that she should monitor her thoughts and feelings for several weeks, and challenge her emotional reactions to the world. On the second occasion, she had been asked to change her eating pattern and monitor her weight. Neither approach helped her to see how all four elements of the hot cross bun tied together (e.g., understanding how her thoughts about weight gain terrified her so much that the idea of eating "normally" was too scary to undertake). Thus, she never learned about how important it was to change her eating slowly, in a way that would help her to challenge her automatic thinking and her emotions and that would help her to regulate her emotional state through improving her carbohydrate intake (see below for details on all of these points). The result was that she quickly gave up any attempt to change and saw herself as a failure and unable to benefit from treatment.

Your journey through CBT: some landmarks

What does CBT involve? We are going to outline the approach here so that you have a broad picture, and then we will fill in the details as the book progresses:
1. First, you will need to learn to identify your problematic behaviors as they happen (e.g., food avoidance, overeating, other linked problems), and to spot the beliefs and emotions that go with them and that can trigger them.

2. Next, CBT involves developing a clear formulation or understanding of *your* problems. While we will consider general models of anorexia and bulimia (i.e., theories that provide a general understanding of how these two disorders work) later on, it is essential that you develop a model that is specific to you (especially as most people with eating disorders do not neatly fit the diagnostic stereotypes). Your model will include all the elements from the "hot cross bun," but might also include issues such as your motivation and your relationships with your family, friends and others. This formulation will serve as a roadmap for how your therapy will help you move on from your eating disorder.

3. Third, you need to learn to change your beliefs and your behaviors, so that you can eat normally.

4. The final step is learning to fully "let go" of the eating problem, so that you can get on with your life. This involves developing more positive life goals, which you may have lost sight of. However, it also means that you will need to identify when you are at risk of relapsing, and how to cope with such pressures.

The rest of this book is about how to develop these skills and use them.

It is worth stating that many sufferers and carers find it hard to believe that going through the process outlined above will be sufficient to help the sufferer improve and recover. This disbelief is understandable, given that many sufferers have had their eating disorder for years or even decades (see the later chapter on motivation, and particularly the "miracle question"), and many will have tried treatments that were not successful. However, we want to stress that we have seen many such individuals make this journey successfully.

What is CBT self-help?

Self-help involves you learning an individualized approach to how to use the right techniques at the right time, so that you can leave your problem behind. However, while the self-help approach is an individualized one, it has some non-negotiables – things that you will have to do in order to make it work.

There are many self-help books available (and CD-ROMs, DVDs and internet-based packages) for a range of emotional problems (e.g., depression, anxiety), including eating concerns. They vary in so many dimensions that it is impossible to detail them here (though some key ones are detailed in the "Further Reading" section of the References, p. 190). This book is specifically about the CBT approach. However, unlike most existing books, it is not about either anorexia or bulimia. In recent years, there has been a growing awareness that anorexia and bulimia have more shared features than differences – that the same thoughts, feelings and behaviors can be found in all such cases – and this book reflects that fact. In fact, over time many people will suffer from different manifestations of their eating disorder. For example, anorexia may develop into bulimia. Working with this knowledge is known as a "transdiagnostic" approach.

We have to stress this point – CBT can work for you, if you put in the work. It has the biggest evidence base for the eating disorders and its effectiveness is at least on a par with every other therapy for anorexia, bulimia and atypical cases. Self-help versions of CBT also have an evidence base in the eating disorders. There is no reason why these benefits should not apply to you. However, CBT will not work unless you do the hard work involved.

CBT is not a rigid, protocol-driven approach where you have to do a set of things in a very specific order. Rather, it is an approach that depends on you learning to apply principles in a way that gives you the best chance of recovery. That flexibility can make CBT seem even harder, as there is a lot of thinking to be done to make it work for you as an individual and for your own eating problem.

There is good evidence that a self-help approach is a good first step towards care for many patients with an eating disorder, with at least a moderate impact on symptoms (e.g., Fairburn & Harrison, 2003). Research studies show that many patients recover completely with this approach. Indeed, many guidelines (e.g., National Institute for Health and Clinical Excellence, 2004) recommend that self-help should be tried first, before undertaking more intensive individual therapy. A large number of specialist clinics recommend using self-help before being considered for one-to-one therapy, or while you are on the waiting list. Indeed, that might be why you have this book in your hands.

The best single predictor of whether CBT will work for you is whether you do the work that we outline in **Sections** **2** and **3**. There is no way round that. You need to have clear goals, and to work towards them.

You will only know if CBT self-help works for *you* by trying it out, as there are no clear guidelines regarding which individuals will do well. If you have tried the approach (rather than simply buying the book) and find that it is not enough, then you might need to get more help, as outlined in **Section 5**. You will need to consider how to find the right help and how to negotiate the transition into formal treatment. This requires you to use an important set of self-help skills – seeking and accepting support. How you handle the transition and how to act as your own therapist once you enter treatment will be very important in how well that additional help is likely to work for you.

An important consideration is how to leave behind a disorder that has been so much a part of your life for so long. While it might seem like an overwhelming problem right now, you should know that this is a skill that many sufferers find they need. So that you have it in mind, remember that **Section 6** of this book is about how to handle that transition. While leaving the eating problem behind might seem a long way away right now, it can be useful to have it in mind from the beginning.

"I'm not sure that I'm ready to change": a quick word about motivation

We will talk more about motivation in the next chapter. However, in case your motivation is already waning, this brief section is just to get you thinking about your reasons for being scared of change, so that you can weigh up the pros and cons of engaging in self-help.

Not everyone wants to change or to give up their eating disorder. This can be for many reasons:

- for some people the eating disorder can feel like part of their identity, and they fear what life would be like if they did not have this to focus on (e.g., "Who would I be if I were not 'the thin one'?")
- sometimes the eating disorder is like a good friend or a security blanket, which you cannot imagine coping without
- sometimes the eating disorder helps you manage difficult emotions, and you are fearful about how you might manage these emotions if you did not have the eating disorder
- at other times it can be terrifying to think about eating normally again – fears of losing control over your weight and shape are very common
- some people would like to get rid of the unpleasant side of the eating disorder (e.g., binge-eating) while retaining other parts (e.g., not having to eat in a healthy pattern or keeping your weight at too low a level), even though experience tells us this is not possible

Not all people want to undertake change at the same rate, and recovery is a journey of different lengths for different people. Therefore, we advise that you try the journey, knowing that you can stop or turn back if you want to. Many sufferers only start to develop optimism when they make their first behavioral changes and find that they do not have the feared consequences (e.g., they find they can eat breakfast without gaining weight). If you never start the journey, you can never find out whether you have the strength to make it. However, if you never start the journey, then you know that the future is likely to be unchanged.

3

How to use this book

Read it all

The first thing that you need to do is to gather information about the task that faces you – so that you can decide if this is something that you want to do at this point in your life. Therefore, you need to read the whole book now, even if parts seem irrelevant at the moment. That will help you to find the helpful parts when you need them. And read it all even if you do not believe that change is possible. It might help you understand that change can happen, and that it makes sense to be optimistic about your being able to get rid of the eating problems.

If you are a sufferer

The key material about doing CBT for yourself is in Chapters 2 and 3. A lot of the appendices will also be helpful to you. And remember that there are many things that you will need to do if you want this to work – the "non-negotiables" of therapy. You might hope that you will get well without having to do them. However, there are no exceptions if you want to give yourself the best chance of getting well and eating normally again.

If you are a carer

If you are a carer, a relative, a partner, or a friend who wants to help a sufferer, then the key material for you is in Chapter 4. The appendices should be useful for you, too.

Whoever you are

If it is time to think about getting more formal help, then the key material is in Chapter 5. However, other sections will be helpful to give you an idea of what to expect in formal care.

For the sufferer

This section is written for the person who has the eating disorder. However, it is also important to share this material with your carers in order to allow them to understand what you will need to do. We will cover the following areas:
- whether you have a problem that deserves consideration
- your motivation to change or stay the same
- making your mind up whether now is the time to do therapy for your eating disorder (balancing your motivation and your current life circumstances)
- getting started with therapy, including planning out what you will need to do

4

Am I making a fuss about nothing?

If you were not concerned about your eating, you would not be reading this book. But do you really have a problem that needs help? Go back to Questionnaire 1a (Chapter 1). If your answers confirm your suspicions that you have a problem with your eating, then read on. To help you with your understanding of eating disorders, there are a number of definitions that it is useful to clarify and a number of myths that it is useful to dispel, so let's start there.

Some important definitions

Diagnosis. When people think about eating disorders among adults, they usually think of either anorexia nervosa or bulimia nervosa. However, the majority of people with an eating disorder do not fit neatly into these diagnoses, but are described as "atypical" cases (also known as Eating Disorder Not Otherwise Specified). This means that you may have some symptoms of either anorexia nervosa or bulimia nervosa, but you do not meet all the criteria for severity, or you may have a much more "mixed" presentation.

Diagnosis is a controversial subject. Some clinicians tend to focus on diagnosis as an aid to communication. However, it is not particularly helpful or necessary to know your exact diagnosis, as it has little link to the type of treatment that you need. In recognition of the fact that very many sufferers (probably most) find themselves in just this situation, we now focus on the thoughts, feelings, biology and behaviors that people with eating disorders have in common, rather than on diagnosis.

Bingeing. Many people with eating disorders binge on food. A binge is when you consume food in a frantic, impulsive way. During the binge itself, you feel out of control, numb and detached. Your focus is narrowed to the food you are eating, with all other experiences (especially negative ones) blocked out of awareness for the duration of the binge.

Bingeing can be divided into two categories, that are determined by the quantity of food that you consume in a single episode. *Objective bingeing* involves the consumption of a very large amount of food (definitely more than others would eat over that space of time). For example, many people binge on 2000–4000 kilocalories[1] in a single sitting, usually in private. In contrast, *subjective bingeing* involves eating far fewer kilocalories (e.g., maybe a single biscuit or a normal meal), while still feeling out of control. In either case, we know that it is the sense of loss of control that matters, and that is central to how you react emotionally and behave (e.g., restricting food, vomiting, exercising). Therefore, we do not treat either form of bingeing as more important, but they will obviously have different effects on issues such as weight gain.

Obesity. Although simple obesity (in the absence of behaviors such as binge-eating) is a serious and distressing problem, it is not treated as part of the constellation of eating disorders. This is because the factors that lead to the development and maintenance of obesity are different from those that lead to an eating disorder, so that treatment for obesity needs to be different too. If you are obese but do not binge or have any of the other behavioral patterns that we talk about here, this book is not for you. There are many resources for helping you with obesity, but it is vital that you focus on one that gives the prospect of slow, long-term change (rather than any kind of "miracle cure" that promises fast results). While you should talk with your doctor about your physical wellbeing, we recommend that you should consider a CBT self-help book focused on weight problems. The book by Gauntlett-Gilbert and Grace (2005) in the references is worth considering.

Myths to dispel

You have to be thin to have an eating disorder. A low weight is only one of many possible symptoms of an eating disorder. Remember that the great majority of people with an eating disorder are in the normal weight range or above. In addition, many of the risk factors to your physical and psychological health are unrelated to low weight. Finally, most individuals with eating disorders tend to see themselves as bigger than they actually are, making your judgement about your size rather questionable anyway (women in general are particularly poor at judging their own size).

Only women have eating disorders. It is true that the majority of those suffering from an eating disorder are women. There are about 20–35 females for every one male with an eating disorder. However, men certainly do experience the same eating problems as women. Women probably experience these disorders more because of society's definitions of "acceptable" appearance and ways for women to deal with emotions (e.g., women using food, men using alcohol or aggression). Such stereotypes can make it particularly hard for men to access help.

---

[1] Please note that one kilocalorie (kcal) is the correct technical term for what most people refer to as one calorie. So, for example, when someone says that they are on a 1500 calories per day diet, the correct term should be 1500 kilocalories. Some countries use joules rather than calories, but we have retained the more common unit in common language.

I must be disturbed to think this way about my eating and my body. Unfortunately, in today's climate it seems to be normal for women to be dissatisfied with the way they look. Dissatisfaction with your body exists on a continuum, but if you have an eating disorder your dissatisfaction goes beyond a simple desire to look slightly different. If you have an eating disorder, the way your body looks can influence every thought and feeling that you have, every decision that you make, and every action that you take. Most importantly, it influences your sense of self-worth, and you start to ignore other ways of evaluating yourself (e.g., career, family, friends, intimate relationships).

Eating disorders are entirely negative. Eating disorders are commonly described in terms of the damage they do and their uncontrollable nature. However, that is not the whole picture, by any means. If eating disorders were entirely negative, then far more sufferers would simply eat normally and leave the problem behind. It is critical to understand the *function* of the eating disorder. Eating behaviors act as a form of coping strategy – providing a way of dealing with the difficult things that life throws at you by "blocking" them out of awareness. Sometimes sufferers do this by focusing on a long-term pattern of behaviors (e.g., restricting eating, over-exercise, checking your weight all the time), and others do it more impulsively (e.g., binge-eating or vomiting when distressed). Finally, a lot of sufferers use both methods at different times. In the short term, this strategy helps by protecting you from distress, but in the long term it creates more difficulties as the problems that are generating the distress are not resolved but instead are left to get worse. The question then is: do I take a short-term risk (and undertake some very hard, emotionally distressing work) by trying to overcome my eating disorder, or do I play safe in the short term by keeping the eating problem (and putting up with the associated long-term pain and inconvenience)? The cinema analogy (below) is worth bearing in mind:

The cinema analogy (Part 1)

Imagine going to the cinema. The film you are watching represents your life. Sometimes it is challenging to watch, frightening or even upsetting. So when someone comes and sits in front of you wearing a large hat you are quite relieved that they have blocked your view. This person represents your eating disorder blocking out difficult thoughts and feelings. However, you still have a partial view of the screen and can still hear the soundtrack clearly, so you know that you are missing what has the potential to be a really good film. Part of you wants the person in front to move, but another part is afraid of what you might see, and feels safer continuing to hide. The longer you sit there, however, watching those around you engrossed in and enjoying the film, the more you feel like you are missing out on something.

Are your attitudes towards eating, shape, and weight serving to protect you from the difficult aspects of your life, but preventing you from achieving your potential? Is your eating disorder blocking your view of the film?

Table 4.1

Disadvantages (cons) of my eating disorder
Physical health/wellbeing
Psychological health/wellbeing (e.g., mood, stress, happiness, ability to think, plan and concentrate)
Family
Friends
Intimate relationships
Personal development (e.g., self-esteem, hobbies/leisure, career, education, future dreams)

We will come back to the cinema analogy later on, when considering the process of deciding whether it is time to change (see Chapter 6).

Ultimately, the best way to determine whether you have an eating disorder that needs addressing is to decide if your attitudes to eating, shape and weight are getting in the way of you living your life the way you want to live it – affecting your thoughts, your emotions, your behaviors, your relationships and your physical wellbeing. To get a clear picture of this possibility, think about each of the following aspects of life and consider whether your eating problems are currently having a negative impact on them. Write the negative aspects (cons) down on the chart above in Table 4.1 (Disadvantages of my eating disorder). It can be very telling if you ask your family, friends or loved ones to complete the same sheet. Often, they can see patterns in your life that are harder for you to see.

5

Motivating yourself to treat your eating disorder

Given that you are reading this book, you will probably have noticed that you have two contradictory ways of thinking about your eating disorder. One part of you has had enough of the fact that every decision you make is influenced by what you eat and/or what you weigh, and would like to get rid of the eating disorder as soon as possible. This part of you is probably what motivated you to read this book in the first place. However, there will be another part of you that would rather not be thinking about this at all. This second part of you may be afraid that you will be asked to make changes that are scary to contemplate (e.g., eating differently, gaining weight, dealing with emotions differently). These two conflicting ways of thinking about your eating disorder can feel confusing, and will make the decision to change very hard to make. Since you are reading this book, it is likely that you have felt "frozen," and unable to get on with your life.

Motivational states

Your motivation to change will fluctuate from one day to another, or even one minute to another. Therefore, there is no point in deciding, "I am ready" or "I just want to be left alone" and expecting to feel the same way the next time you think about it. The next box lists a commonly defined set of "states" in the motivation of sufferers, giving the labels, definitions, and ways in which this book can help you move towards recovery. Because people tend to fluctuate across these patterns of motivation in very individual ways, we tend to think of them as "states" rather than "stages" (where there is an implication that you will pass through them in a predictable order). Remember that you can move between these states, and do not be disappointed if you feel that your progress is not always maintained. To be effective, the treatment that you are undertaking needs to match the motivational state that you are in. If it does

Motivational states that are common in eating disorders

Anti-contemplation (e.g., "There is nothing wrong – how dare you suggest there is!")
- Sufferers in this state are not able to think about even having a problem. This can be the case even where there is very substantial damage and risk (both physically and psychologically). If the individual recognizes that she or he has a problem of any sort (e.g., being substantially under-weight), she or he may spend a long, fruitless time seeking other causes (e.g., physical causes such as food allergies, thyroid problems) and resisting any suggestion that there is an eating disorder per se. Because those around the sufferer *can* see a problem and often express strong concerns, arguments can ensue. This is the state that can be the most frustrating for carers.
- This book is highly unlikely to be read by a sufferer who is regularly in this state. However, it is more likely to be used by a carer who is trying to find ways of helping the sufferer (see Section 4 p. 95).

Pre-contemplation (e.g., "I'm not ready to change")
- In this state, you are not ready to contemplate a change at present, though you can see that it might be necessary in the future. Your reluctance to move now might be owing to your lack of knowledge about the detrimental impact of your eating disorder on your physical and psychological health. Alternatively, you might feel that your life circumstances are too chaotic, unstable or challenging for you to be able to consider changing what feels like your only coping strategy.
- If you are pre-contemplative, this book might be useful in considering if now is the time to move on towards change. It will provide you with important information about keeping yourself as safe as possible, both physically and psychologically.

Contemplation (e.g., "I'm thinking about change")
- In this state, you are ready to take in more information about the possibility of change, and you are likely to be more interested in the idea of change in general. This often manifests as considering possible plans (e.g., thinking what you would like to have different in your life over the next six months), but without acting to make them possible (e.g., thinking that you might like children in the future, but not making any firm decision). You are more aware of the disadvantages of your eating disorder and the advantages of resolving it, but another part of you is still very afraid of this.
- This book can help you to start thinking about why your eating disorder has developed, why it has not resolved itself, the longer-term consequences on your life if it continues, and what you could do in the future to resolve it.

Preparation (e.g., "I'm getting ready for change")
- If you are in this state, you have made the decision to change and intend to act shortly (e.g., in the next month). In this state you will be developing a plan of action (e.g., devising a regular eating plan, recruiting friends and family for support, getting a referral for treatment). Good planning at this point will optimize your chances of successful recovery (see Chapter 8).
- This book can help you to gather the knowledge and take the steps to maximize your chances of successfully resolving your eating disorder.

Action (e.g., "I'm starting to change")
- This is the state where you begin to make changes. However, it is important to remember that this is not the first step in the process of change, but that other things (particularly contemplation and planning) must come first. The most common mistake that people can make in the change process is jumping to take action before they are ready.
- This book can guide you through a self-help program to recovery. You can get the most benefit by reading on from here.

Maintenance (e.g., "I'm making changes and hanging in there")
- This is the state where you are working to consolidate changes, prevent relapse and continue your personal development.
- This book can help you to consolidate your recovery, guard against relapse and move you forward in your personal development.

not, the treatment will make you feel anxious, frustrated and more stuck. Take a look at the definitions, and consider how they each relate to your current state (and what you might do about it, using this book). Remember, you might see different parts of yourself as being in different states at the same time.

The pros and cons of having an eating disorder

At the end of Chapter 4, we considered the disadvantages of having your eating problem. While there are obviously lots of such disadvantages (the cons) to having an eating disorder (emotional problems, physical risk, social withdrawal, etc.), it is important to remember that there will also be good points to the "problem" (the pros). In fact, many people with eating disorders see the eating disorder as a solution, rather than a problem. So let's think about a couple of the biggest pros:

- *Feeling in control.* An eating disorder can help you feel as if you are in control in at least one area of your life. Even if you are bingeing, vomiting or using other behaviors that make you feel out of control, resolving to re-start your diet again gives you a short-term sense of calm and control (and the promise of longer-term control and happiness, if you can just manage to stick to it this time and lose some weight).
- *Sense of achievement.* If you manage to lose some weight, an eating disorder can also provide you with a short-term sense of achievement, and may feel like the only thing you have managed or can achieve. People with eating disorders often say that they feel worthless, but at least they feel thin and worthless.

Such pros are why part of you does not want to give up your eating disorder. It is important to be clear about the pros of *your* eating disorder, so that you know exactly what you will be giving up if you decide to change, what gaps will need to be filled, and what coping strategies will need to be replaced. The next step is to expand on the previous list, to consider the pros as well as the cons of your disorder. Think about what is positive and what is negative about *your* eating disorder, and fill in Table 5.1.

It is quite likely that you found more "cons" than "pros" in your list. However, rather than just saying: "Well, why can't I stop doing this?" it is important to consider just how powerful those pros must be. Often, the pros are about short-term benefits, and you hold on to them in order to deal with the panicky feelings that you get when thinking about giving them up. For example, you might feel calmer after checking yourself in the mirror, even though you know that you end up feeling more worried about your weight long term, but the fear about what would happen to your weight if you stopped this checking is too strong.

Table 5.1

Area of my life	Pros of my eating disorder	Cons of my eating disorder (see earlier table)
Physical health/wellbeing		
Psychological health/wellbeing (e.g., mood, stress, memory, concentration)		
Family		
Friends		
Intimate relationships (e.g., sex life, having children)		
Personal development (e.g., self-esteem, hobbies/leisure, career, education)		

In short, it is often the case that people with eating disorders trade the short-term comfort of not having to change for the long-term frustration of staying stuck with the eating disorder. This way of looking at and responding to things will come up in the next section under the label of "safety behaviors." What is needed is a clear idea of what you would gain long term by facing your anxieties about change. This is by no means an easy thing to implement.

Therefore, to get that bigger picture, the next step is to take the pros and cons that you have outlined in the previous table (Table 5.1), and to divide them up into short- and long-term pros and cons. You can do that in the next table (Table 5.2). For example, if you restrict your food intake and you put "Feeling happier" into the "advantages pros" box, then consider whether the restriction makes you feel happier in the short term, but leaves you feeling more miserable and fearful long term. Likewise, you might feel that a good point about bulimia in the short term is that it means that you do not have to let anyone get close and find the "real" you, but long term you have no chance to develop a supportive relationship. Do this for all the pros and cons that you identified above, and add others if you think of them as you go along.

What do you notice about the distribution of advantages and disadvantages across time? Very often, we find that sufferers have a lot of short-term pros and lots of long-term cons (lots of entries in the top left part of the table and in the bottom right part, but fewer in the top right and bottom left). If this is how

Table 5.2

	Area of my life	Advantages of my eating disorder (pros)	Disadvantages of my eating disorder (cons)
Short term (minutes/hours/ days/ weeks)	Physical health/wellbeing Psychological health/wellbeing Family Friends Intimate relationships Personal development		
Long term (months/years)	Physical health/wellbeing Psychological health/wellbeing Family Friends Intimate relationships Personal development		

things are for you, then what this tells you is that you are trading in lots of your future development in order to get short-term relief. Are you happy to buy five minutes of calm, even if it means years of misery? What would you advise a friend to do in that situation? Is now the time to act in order to change your life, and not just your eating?

6

Is now the time to act?

While everyone around you might be thinking that the answer to this question is obvious, you probably do not. Even if you can say that you want to change, actually doing it is a lot harder. The reason is the short-term benefits that we discussed in the previous chapter – your eating disorder has a positive element that keeps you stuck. So what do you need to think about when deciding whether to go from contemplation and preparation into action (see motivational states – Chapter 5)? We find that there need to be three general considerations – your general life circumstances, the balance between the pros and cons of your eating disorder, and where you place the responsibility for change.

Life circumstances

If it's going to work, therapy takes a lot of time and commitment. You need to consider your other commitments and demands on your time (e.g., work and family), as well as the support that is available to you within your social/family network. You will need a certain amount of stability here. If the stability is not there already, then how might you make things more stable? How might your family, friends and carers help in this? It is very easy and tempting to say "I will wait until life is calmer, and then change," but will life get any calmer in the foreseeable future? Is it going to be possible to find an easier time, or will you have to make the space to do this work?

The balance between the pros and cons of your eating disorder

Change of any sort is difficult, even changes that seem as if they would be easy at first glance. For example, for someone who is keen to learn to play tennis, increase their fitness, and expand their social network, it might seem obvious that the next step is to join a tennis club. However, even a change with so many obvious and relatively immediate benefits can create challenges – the demands of learning a new skill, meeting new people, the physical strain of a new exercise on the body, and (perhaps above all) the risk of failure.

The longer it will take to achieve the goals, the harder it can be to make the investment of time and effort that will be necessary to get there. Therefore, it is important that the cons of the eating disorder outweigh the pros sufficiently to make all this hard work worthwhile. To make sure of this, you need to see your eating disorder as something that is both comforting in the short term and damaging in the long term. The following analogy of the itchy jumper is a good one to keep in mind:

The itchy jumper

Your eating disorder is like a cheap jumper. When you first put it on, it keeps you nice and warm. However, it is not made out of very good wool, and so after a while it starts to itch. Sometimes you might feel like taking it off, but you know that if you do you will be cold, so you put up with the itchiness. With time, however, the itchiness gets harder and harder to tolerate. The jumper gets more and more uncomfortable, and although it still keeps you warm, you start to wonder whether there might be better ways of keeping yourself warm.

If you decide the time has come to take off your jumper, it is important first to explore the other ways that you might be able to keep yourself warm (the "*planning*" state of change). However, at some point you will have to take the itchy jumper off and be cold for a period while you try out other ways of keeping warm. This may feel more uncomfortable in the short term, but in the longer term it will allow you to keep warm in an itch-free way.

If you don't feel able at present to change your eating behaviors, this might be because your jumper has not yet become itchy enough for you to want to risk being cold. If this is the case, you may have to continue wearing your jumper for a bit longer. At the same time, however, it could be helpful to explore other ways that you can keep warm – maybe ones that you can practice while still wearing your itchy jumper.

Accepting responsibility for change

When we feel stuck in a position where we are struggling, a common response is to conclude that responsibility for change lies outside of ourselves – either other people have to change or the world as a whole has to change before we can. Someone else should find you a less itchy jumper, or all jumpers should be changed so that they are no longer itchy. In the short term, such a response allows you to avoid the challenge and discomfort that would be involved if you concluded that you had to initiate a change. However, in the long term, placing responsibility for change anywhere other than with yourself means that you will inevitably be stuck in that uncomfortable position (the itchy jumper will only be changed if you change it). This is true whether you are engaged in self-help or working with a therapist directly – you have to change your behavior and take risks before any other improvement can happen.

You might reason that the eating disorder has a biological or genetic component, and that this makes change beyond your control. However, although there is evidence of a biological–genetic element in the complex causality and maintenance of eating disorders, there is no evidence that such factors prevent you from benefiting from treatment. You still have the choice of changing.

The foundation of treating your eating disorder is being honest with yourself – accepting that only you can make this choice for you, and only you can initiate the action that has to follow on from this choice. This is not to say that the choice is an easy one, or that the action will not be challenging at times, or that you can do it without help. However, accepting responsibility for what happens to you and for getting started on the path you need to take is key if you want to move forward. Only when you are ready to accept this responsibility will you be able to decide that this is the right time to change. Let us take the cinema analogy (Chapter 4) to the next level.

The cinema analogy (Part 2)

Deciding to undertake therapy means that you have to be able to give your full attention to the task, rather like watching a movie when you have decided that you really want to see it. So you have decided that you want to see the film and be able to give it your full attention. You have paid for and chosen a good seat. But then someone come and sits right in front of you, wearing a hat and blocking your view of the film. You have two options if you still want to see the film:
- You could move seats. This is the equivalent of giving up when there is a problem, and avoiding it rather than overcoming it. It means that you get your view of the film back, but you are less comfortable, and you are vulnerable to yet another person sitting in front of you, blocking your view, and requiring you to move again. Eventually, as you become more used to avoiding problems of this sort, you spend all your time finding new seats and worrying about the next person who is going to come into the cinema. You may even run out of seats to go to. Your experience of the film is ruined by the need to deal with problems by avoiding them.
- You could ask the person in front to remove their hat. This ensures that you are able to watch the film uninterrupted. However, it requires you to have confidence in your own capacity to make changes, as well as the courage to carry out the actions needed to achieve them (including dealing with other's reactions to your needs and actions).

So which will you choose? Will you be brave enough to make the scary changes that allow you to benefit long term, or will you duck out of them and end up feeling that your time has been wasted?

The itchy jumper analogy emphasizes the fact that no one else can make this happen. While you will undoubtedly need help to change (see the following chapters), simply wanting things to change will not make it so. You will have to be an active participant in the process to ensure your own recovery. That might include recruiting others to assist you (family, friends, carers, clinicians), but their efforts will not help if you expect to be able to give up all personal responsibility for change.

7

Getting started with CBT

So you have decided to take the step of changing from your current ways of coping (using eating behaviors that help you to cope in the short term by making you feel safe, but which cripple your life in the long term) into a more helpful way of coping (which will be scary in the short term, but which might allow you to get your life back in the long term). How can you turn this into a reality?

The main tasks to help you achieve this goal are outlined in the next section – the CBT self-help workbook. However, before you undertake them, you will need to think about (and act on) the following:

- taking on the role of becoming "your own therapist"
- having realistic expectations about what can and what can't be achieved (taking the rough with the smooth)
- maximizing your chances of success by making it your priority to overcome your eating problem

Becoming your own therapist

An underlying goal of CBT is to help you become your own therapist. Your chances are naturally much better if you work at this task 24 hours a day, seven days per week, than if you let it flit in and out of awareness. Therefore, you have to keep yourself aware of the tasks of therapy all the time – even when you are getting on with the rest of your life – rather than only focusing on it when you have the time.

We aim to teach you practical and psychological skills that will enable you to choose healthier ways of coping with life – ways that won't undermine your health and happiness in the way that your eating disorder currently does. This is why both having the motivation to change and taking responsibility for change is so fundamental to resolving your eating disorder. Through CBT you can move forward in the way that you choose, but only if you are an active and keen participant in the process. Cognitive behavioral therapy is "practical" therapy, teaching you a set of skills that you then have responsibility for implementing.

The river analogy that follows is useful to remind you that you have to make active choices in change.

The river analogy

When you suffer from an eating disorder, it is as if you are being swept along by a fast-flowing river. All your energy goes on simply keeping afloat – clinging to floating debris, treading water, etc. All of these activities will probably keep you from harm (in the short term), but you remain at the mercy of the river, its current and its course. You are swept along with little or no say in the direction that you go. Many people hope that treatment will be like a powerful speed boat that pulls you from the water to safety. However, although this would mean that you would be out of the water, you would still not be where you wanted to be, and you would not have learned the skills to get yourself there. Control would have shifted, but not in a positive direction.

Cognitive behavioral therapy aims to get you to a better place, but will involve making choices and learning how to get where you want to be. In order to do this, the first step in CBT is to help you to swim to the edge of the river and climb onto the bank (even though this particular spot will not be where you want to end up). From this vantage point, you can see a more complete range of options – options that were hard to see when you were struggling to survive in the river. You now have time to think about where you want to end up and how to get there. That might involve building a boat, walking rather than floating, looking for a bridge, or even traveling away from the river altogether. Alternatively, you might decide not to do anything about it and return to being carried along by the river, but you will be doing so with a full awareness of the other options that are available to you (and knowing that you could get out again in the future and reconsider those options).

So, by teaching you the practical and psychological skills needed to overcome your eating disorder, this book will enable you to reach a greater understanding of your eating as a coping mechanism and the other options that are available to you. It will help you take a step back from your eating disorder and become your own therapist, standing on the bank of the river and then liberating you to be able to determine the course your life takes in future.

What to expect

Changing your eating disorder is not a smooth process. First, it means giving up your short-term coping mechanisms (including many "pros" of the eating disorder) without being sure that you will learn how to feel good about yourself in the long run. This often means a period of anxiety (e.g., "How on earth can

I possibly eat more without losing control of my weight?") that you will have to tolerate for long enough to find out if it is true that you can cope differently. Second, you will have to focus on the eating disorder and all the problems that underlie it. This can be distressing, because we will be asking you to do the opposite of what you are used to doing (i.e., what you feel safe and comfortable with).

Given all this, we can make one prediction that will apply to nearly anyone with an eating disorder who uses this book:

You are going to feel worse before you feel better

Indeed, if you do not experience some anxiety and distress when you begin to change, you are probably not doing CBT correctly (and hence you are probably not going to benefit from this program). There are no short cuts. So make sure that you warn your carers and those around you that you might need some help with dealing with these feelings – better to do this than to hide those feelings if you really want to recover, because hiding the feelings will make you doubt your ability to change. You will still have bad days, but the bad days will become less frequent, and when they do occur they will be less intense and easier to resolve.

To summarize: in the short term you will have to tolerate many of the disadvantages of change, while you can see few of the advantages. It is only when you continue with change that you will get the long-term benefits that come with resolving your eating disorder. The following "Coast of South America" analogy is worth thinking about as you start the change process, and you should return to it as you go along.

Giving yourself the best chance of success

Before you start your CBT program, there are things that you can do to maximize your chances of success. First, you will have to learn to treat yourself as a priority, rather than seeing everybody else's needs as more important than yours. Second, you will need to set yourself achievable goals, so that you can tell when you are succeeding and when you need to change your tactics to be able to keep making progress.

Prioritizing yourself and your recovery. As we have discussed, for CBT to enable you to overcome your eating disorder, you need to be a keen and active participant in the process. This will take time and energy. Therefore, you will need to prioritize both yourself and your recovery, and to maintain this for weeks and months. Prioritizing yourself like this can be difficult, particularly if you have a low sense of self-worth. The steps outlined below will help you approach the task in a practical and determined way – including enabling you to challenge any tendency to put other's needs ahead of your own.

- *Step 1: Anticipate and prepare for obstacles.* If you can anticipate the obstacles to change, it gives you the opportunity to prepare solutions/coping strategies, and to choose the best solution rather than the first one that you think of. Such obstacles to change will include both emotional ones (e.g., anxiety about

The coast of South America

One way to think about the process of recovery from an eating disorder is to think of a trek along the coastline of South America (if you are not a geographer, you might want to find an atlas or a map at this point). You had initially hoped to travel from west coast to east coast by car, taking a smooth eastbound road across the center of the country, but you are told at the last minute that there is no car and that there is no such road anyway. Instead you must walk, setting off in what intuitively seems like the wrong direction – the equivalent of starting in Chile and then heading down to the southernmost tip of South America (heading south rather than east). As you round the southern tip of the continent, you begin to feel as if you are starting to go the right way (beginning to trek north east up the coast of Argentina). From time to time the coastal path will take you inland away from the coastline, and you will feel as if you are diverting from the correct path. However, if you keep moving, following the signs pointed out by your guides, you will eventually reach your desired destination. But would you undertake this sort of journey without a map and a guide to reassure you that you are on the right path (and to tell you when you are going wrong)?

The trek along the coastline of South America can also be used to think about the CBT goal of becoming your own therapist. During the first phase of your trek, your guide (this book) will teach you the various skills you need for your journey, taking the lead through the sometimes challenging terrain. However, as you become a more accomplished trekker/therapist, you will begin to feel more confident about taking the lead. Although when you have finished this book, you may not have completely resolved your eating disorder, you will feel in a much stronger position to continue your journey along the coastline to recovery independently.

weight gain, lack of alternative ways of coping with emotions) and practical ones (e.g., other commitments and demands on your time). We suggest that you start now by completing the two columns below (Table 7.1) – identify all the things that could happen that would get in the way of your changing over the next few months (maybe specific events, like Christmas, and maybe things that are more about other's behavior and your coping style), and then start to think about ways that you could overcome those obstacles. If you have trouble with the "Solutions" list, then think about what you would recommend that a friend should do to cope with exactly the same stressors and obstacles.

- *Step 2: Monitor your physical health.* As we have already said, your eating disorder might be putting your physical health at risk. Therefore, before you do anything, make an appointment to see your doctor so that they can assess and monitor your physical health. Let them know that you are planning to try a self-help CBT approach, and that you need to be sure you are physically safe

Table 7.1

Obstacles to change	Solutions to obstacles

first (as any good CBT approach would stress if you were going to do this work with a clinician rather than on your own).

- *Step 3: Develop a support network.* Eating disorders can trigger a lot of guilt and shame. As a result, you may find that you have withdrawn from other people, hiding your true thoughts, feelings and behaviors for fear that others will judge you negatively. In the absence of other ways of coping, this hiding is an understandable response, but it will leave you feeling more overwhelmed, isolated, and stuck. This book offers you a different way of coping but, as we have discussed, the journey to recovery is challenging. It is therefore important that you have as much support as possible. Discuss what you read in this book with your partner, carers, friends or others, as much as you can (even if you start only by asking them to read it). If you do not have anyone who can support you in this way, then have you considered talking to others who have experienced an eating problem? You can use the resources listed in Appendix 1 to find that sort of support for yourself. (However, you need to be careful not to fall into the trap of ending up being the support for others at this stage.)

- *Step 4: Be appropriately assertive.* If your needs are not met, you will be left feeling deprived, isolated, and uncared for. A key part of your recovery will be to get your needs met. This will feel both unfamiliar and uncomfortable, because you are not used to focusing on yourself in this way. To learn to do this, you must first identify what you need. Then you must work out who can provide it. If you have a tendency to sacrifice yourself for others, you may have people around you who do not have the capacity to meet your needs. If this is the case you will have to look outside of these relationships, possibly distancing yourself from them in order to move forward. Finally, you will need to communicate what you need. Being appropriately assertive is a skill, and like all skills it needs to be practiced and given time to develop. This book can help you do this, but as a first step you need to place yourself in the center of your own priorities.

Setting goals. Setting goals will guide you towards your destination (recovery), keep you on track and help you to measure your progress along the way. When you keep measuring your progress in this way, you can decide when you are still doing well and when you need to change tactics.

Sometimes, you need to think about your overall, longer-term goals (e.g., living a normal life, having a family of your own, developing a career) before you can start to decide whether it is worth undertaking the shorter-term tasks of changing your eating. However, when you have had an eating disorder for an extended period of time, it can be hard to imagine how life would be without it. Not knowing exactly what you are aiming for can make it hard to continue heading in the right direction, especially when the journey is demanding anyway. So it can be helpful to clarify this in your own mind before you start. This image can also keep you going when things get tough. Try asking yourself the "miracle question" (below), and see what your answer would be.

The miracle question

Imagine that when you go to bed tonight a miracle occurs and your eating disorder disappears. However, because you were asleep you do not know that this has happened. Write about the day after the miracle, from the moment that you wake up to when you go to bed at night. Think about what you would do and what others would notice that would make you think that the miracle had occurred. Be as detailed as possible.

The following ("My miracle morning") is an answer that one woman gave to the miracle question. She was surprised at how far her life had gotten away from where she wanted to be. She used her answers to start being clear about her problems (which you can lose perspective on when you are living a life that is so tied up with your eating) and setting personal goals for her treatment.

My miracle morning

I would wake up at a normal time, not in the middle of the night because my stomach hurt. I would be happy, looking forward to the day, instead of being scared about what I was going to be made to eat and about what arguments there were going to be about food. In fact, I probably wouldn't even be thinking about food. I would be back in the house I shared with friends at university, not living with my father and stepmother. I would get up and have a shower and get dressed, just putting on the first outfit I saw, and not checking in the mirror for ages and trying out all clothes in my wardrobe to see what made me look least fat. As I walk downstairs, the first thing my housemates would notice about me is I look well and happy. I sit down for breakfast and don't rush off for a run. I would be happy to see my friends and to chat with them and my head wouldn't be so full of thoughts about food and weight. I would be normal.

Now try answering the miracle question for yourself.

Having identified your specific problems, you can start to set out some specific, concrete, and measurable goals that you can achieve. The next table (Table 7.2) gives an example of the problems identified by a sufferer who had restricted and

Table 7.2

Problems	Goals
Binge-eating – I hate the loss of control and the secrecy	• To stop bingeing and eat normally • To understand why I keep bingeing • To cut down the urge to binge
Vomiting – it's disgusting, my throat hurts and I feel exhausted all the time	• To stop vomiting
Dividing food into "safe" and "unsafe" foods, only feeling comfortable eating a limited number of "safe" foods, and avoiding too many foods that I used to enjoy	• To eat a normal diet (which is a mix of healthy and less healthy foods) without worrying • To start eating avoided foods, including takeaways
Checking my thighs several times a day to ensure they haven't got bigger	• To stop body-checking • To be less concerned with my shape and weight
Feeling like a success or a failure depending on whether I've gained or lost weight	• To gain a more realistic perspective and to experience achievement through other means (e.g., relationships, career)
Don't have enough time for hobbies, family, and friends	• Rejoin my netball team (for healthy, social activity) • Make an effort to improve relationships with family and friends

Table 7.3

Problems	Goals

used bulimic behaviors for many years, and the goals that she was able to identify that would help her feel that she had overcome the problems.

Now make up a list of your own in the table above (Table 7.3).

- Start with the problems in the left hand column, and then start to fill in the goals that you would need to achieve to overcome them.
- Leave lots of space in the right hand column for each of the problems in the left hand column, so that you can add in new goals when you come to see them.
- If you cannot think of goals, then try:
  - asking other people whom you trust to suggest possible goals
  - imagining that it was a friend or relative of yours who was asking you to help them to work out such goals (remember that you are a priority – treat yourself as being as much of a priority as other people)
- Make the goals as specific as possible (e.g., not "Going out more", but "Going out with friends at least twice a week"), so that you can identify clearly at a later stage whether you have been able to achieve them or not. This "measurablility" is also important because we are human, and humans sometimes forget things and lose their sense of perspective. As you progress and start living a more enjoyable life, it can be hard to remember how bad things were, and that means that you cannot see how far you have come. If you cannot see how far you have come, then you cannot give yourself the pat on the back that you deserve when you need it.

Develop alternative coping strategies: self-soothing. So you have identified your problems and your goals. However, the transition is not going to be an easy one. Your eating disorder has been your coping mechanism for a long time. Giving up your eating disorder means you may feel that you are without a way of coping with difficult and challenging experiences. Therefore, it is important that you start developing alternative ways of coping with the world.

As you develop a more positive, less eating-centered way of living, your coping strategies will become more similar to those used by others around you – when you see a problem coming, you will identify it and take steps to head it off before it becomes unmanageable. Over time, your growing self-esteem will allow you to see yourself as more in control of your life, and this will make coping easier. However, you are going to need coping strategies for this interim period – ways of feeling safe and in control while your emotions are at their most raw. This means that you will need to learn to nurture and soothe yourself in a positive way – probably a new experience that doesn't fit with your low sense of self-worth, so it is something else that you will need to dedicate time and practice to. Each time you hit a potentially distressing situation and cope with it without using your eating, you make it easier to repeat that experience next time. You also make it possible to think of ways of making it less likely that the distress will come back.

An effective way of soothing yourself during times of distress is to stimulate one or more of your senses in a positive way. The table below (Table 7.4) gives some examples of alternative ways of coping with distress in this way. You can try them out, but you can also think of additional healthy coping strategies that may be more in line with your own needs and preferences. It is a good idea to practice these healthy ways of coping when there is no crisis, so that you can discover which ones you find most soothing. Think about it – would you ask someone to learn to ride a bicycle in heavy traffic or in the rain, or would you teach them under calmer conditions? So practice these methods when you are feeling calm and when there is no stress (you might need to make the time to do this – remember to prioritize your needs). Once these have become highly practiced skills, you will be able to initiate a soothing activity quickly when you are feeling distressed. Focus on one sense at a time at first, and then practice doing more than one at a time.

Summary

If you have been doing all that we have suggested in this section, you will be ready to move on to the next section – the self-help CBT program itself. But remember, all the work that you have done here has to be carried on throughout your recovery. Think of all the work you have done here as the foundations for the treatment program itself. So far, you should have done all the following:

- decided that you have a problem that deserves consideration and that you deserve to help yourself
- worked on your motivation to change
- considered why now is a good time to start therapy for your eating disorder
- done the preparatory work of becoming your own therapist, knowing what to expect, setting goals, and learning how to cope with the emotional stress of getting by without using your eating problem to deal with life

Table 7.4

Ways of soothing yourself when you are stressed

Vision:
- Focus on nature: take a scenic walk, focus on the vibrant colours of plants/flowers around you, watch fish swimming in a tank/pond, watch birds flying, etc.
- Focus on art: watch a ballet/dance performance, go to a museum with beautiful art
- Decorate a room with all of your best/favourite things

Hearing:
- Listen to music
- Sing/hum to music
- Pay attention to the sounds of nature (water, birds, rainfall, leaves rustling)
- Talk to others (but not anyone who is going to make demands on you – make a list of people around you who are supportive and don't judge you)

Smell:
- Burn incense or an aromatic candle
- Spray your favourite perfume
- Boil cinnamon
- Make fresh coffee
- Smell flowers

Taste:
- Have a soothing drink
- Suck a peppermint
- Treat yourself to food you wouldn't usually spend money on (*N.B. This can be a difficult sensation to work with initially, and so you might want to leave using it until eating has become less emotion-driven*)

Touch:
- Have a bath
- Put clean sheets on your bed
- Put a big warm jumper/silky blouse on
- Put on body lotion
- Wash your hair with nice-smelling products
- Have a massage
- Stroke a cat, dog, rabbit, or other animal

All of the above are important initial steps to recovery, and ones that you will need to keep in mind throughout your recovery. You should think of this work as the foundations for the treatment program itself. Therefore, make sure that you revisit these points during your forthcoming "personal therapy" sessions.

Remember the following key points about CBT:
- CBT gives you a way of understanding your experience that allows you to make robust and enduring changes to your eating. It does this by breaking your experience down into four components (thoughts, feelings, physical states and behaviors), and then implementing practical and psychological changes that address all four of those components

- For CBT to work, you must be motivated to make changes to your current thoughts, physical state, feelings and behaviors
- CBT is not a "miracle cure," but involves you learning to become your own therapist and resolve your problems yourself
- CBT will help you to achieve your goals for change, but you must identify those goals and hold them in mind
- CBT is likely to lead to a short-term increase in your distress levels – you need to remember that this is natural as you learn a new way of coping with anything, and it will allow you to develop much better physical and psychological wellbeing in the longer term.

The CBT self-help program

If you are keen to get to the part where we tell you about the key tasks you need to complete to recover from your eating disorder, you might find the next few pages frustrating and be tempted to skim over them. This is understandable as you might have been suffering from your eating disorder for a long time. However, it is precisely because you have been suffering for some time that you need to read the next section carefully and thoroughly. Eating disorders are complex problems. If they weren't, you would have been able to resolve yours a long time ago. The pages that follow have been written to help you prepare for your recovery – to stop you wading in before you are ready. In a sense, they are a "warm up," which will maximize your chances of resolving your eating disorder once and for all.

8

Start here: how to use this program

Let's start by going back to the three sufferers whom we talked about in Chapter 1 – Jenny, Katy and Polly. You might want to re-read their stories, in order to think about how they got stuck as they were, and to remind yourself of any parallels with your own situation and your eating problem. We will come back to these three sufferers to illustrate points that we make while talking about what they had to do in order to make their treatment work.

- Jenny is a woman who feels stuck in life because of her anorexia – it has tied her down so that she has not been able to develop, partly because her fears have taken all her time and attention. However, her fear of change means that she has stuck with the anorexia so far.
- Katy is younger, and bulimic. Like Jenny, she has lots of anxiety about gaining weight if she eats normally, and that fear means that she is using a range of ways of calming herself (e.g., alcohol, self-harm, restriction, exercise, body checking). She is bingeing when she is too hungry or too upset.
- Polly is older than the other two women. Her concerns about eating, weight, and shape have been around for a very long time, and she deals with those anxieties by eating a limited range of foods (what she calls "safe" foods) and by vomiting when she has broken her own rules. She is feeling that her eating difficulties are seriously affecting her life (her children have started copying her; difficulties at work), but her fear of change has prevented her doing anything about these consequences.

What do these three sufferers have in common? Their eating difficulties center around their eating, weight, and shape concerns. They see good and bad points in their eating. They use a range of eating behaviors that make them feel safer (e.g., restricting, bingeing) in the short term but that get in the way of healthy eating and healthy living in the long term. And they are terrified of what would happen if they just started eating normally.

By this point, we hope that these experiences sound familiar to you. If so, then this CBT program has the potential to help you.

If you are a sufferer

First, we recommend that you read this whole section as if it were not about you. Try to imagine it was something that you were going to recommend to a friend, and you wanted to be sure you were clear about what you were going to suggest that they did. This will ensure that you get a clear idea about what is coming up, realize how much hard work it will be, see what the endpoint could be, and then sit back and decide if the benefits of following the program would outweigh the costs. Discuss it with your carer(s), if you choose to involve them. Finally, come back to this page, and get started. But make sure that you start with the intention of finishing. That means understanding the practicalities, and being willing to put aside any times when you have tried to get better by trying a different approach. It is worth treating all of this approach as being new to you, even if you have tried bits of it before, as the whole program has a better chance of working than all of its parts tried at different times.

If you are a carer (friend, relative, parent, partner)

We recommend that you read this whole section in full. Think about the impact it will have on the sufferer, and how much work is involved. Put yourself in their shoes. Think about the hard work and the anxiety there will be for everyone while they follow this program. Discuss it with the sufferer. If it is possible, then treat it as a problem to solve collaboratively – what can we all do to make this work?

Practicalities

Before you get started on this work, it is vital that you are clear about what you will need to do, and that you have had the time to think about how you will make this all happen. Doing this program will mean dedicating yourself to getting well. However, it will also mean coping with the anxiety that is inevitable when you change from your current pattern of eating to a new, healthier style. Think about Jenny, Katy and Polly – all of them were caught in the trap of being scared of changing, no matter how uncomfortable they were at the time. Just remember:

- simply owning this book (or any other) will not deal with your eating problem. You need to read it and use it.
- changing your behavior is essential, but scary. Anxiety is something that you are going to need to understand, predict, accept, and learn to cope with.

So let's consider why you are going to be anxious, and how your ways of coping with it are likely to be part of the problem.

Anxiety and safety behaviors

If you remember, in Chapter 5 we talked about "safety behaviors." This is where those patterns become most relevant, as we discuss the anxiety involved in changing your eating behavior.

At the heart of your problem is likely to be a powerful belief that eating normally will have a negative effect on you. Maybe you are afraid that your weight will go out of control, that you will never be able to stop eating and gaining weight? Maybe you fear that other people will think you are unacceptable? Maybe you worry that you will start to binge and need to vomit more often if you give in to your hunger? Maybe you are concerned your life will be empty without the eating disorder? Safety behaviors are ways in which you are likely to be responding to fears in an effort to keep yourself safe. These usually involve:

- avoiding the feared place or object (e.g., avoiding someone who you think may be angry with you; never going somewhere that makes you nervous, such as a place where you were once attacked)
- running away (e.g., backing off fast when someone confronts you about the eating problem)
- using other means of blocking things out (e.g., using alcohol to cope with anxiety when going out with friends)
- soothing your fears by checking and taking steps to keep your weight down

In all of these situations, the safety behavior is something that lets you reduce the immediate anxiety. However, because you run away when you are at your most anxious, you still see the feared object as terrifying, and you end up feeling that you only escaped by the skin of your teeth. In other words, in the short term you reduce your anxiety, but in the longer term you actually make it worse because you never give yourself the chance to learn that you can cope, so you end up being just as anxious (or more so) when you next encounter the thing that you are afraid of. So, for example, someone who has an eating problem might use all kinds of safety behaviors, such as:

- Avoidance: never going to restaurants; never deciding what to eat; sticking to very low-kilocalorie foods; avoiding carbohydrates or fats; avoiding finding out your weight; avoiding relationships; avoiding comments on your appearance or body shape by dressing in ways that hide your body
- Running away: starting to eat then stopping; vomiting to avoid weight gain
- Blocking: drinking alcohol; exercising to reduce hunger; focusing on work/ studies rather than eating
- Compensating: checking your body, weighing yourself, exercising to lose the weight that you fear you have gained

Take some time to think about what your safety behaviors are. Just think of them as ways of behaving that make you less anxious in the short term, but that have the potential to make things worse for you in the long term.

Go back to Chapter 1 and think about the safety behaviors that were used by the three women in the case studies. Jenny uses dieting and exercise to reduce her fear that her weight is going to shoot up out of control. In the very short term, she feels calmer when she does these things. In the long term, her anxiety returns in the form of concerns about eating anything at all (which she cannot avoid), and her body is suffering. Katy uses restriction, alcohol and self-harm to control her anxiety about weight gain and her fears about how others will see her, but ends up feeling worse about herself and less in control, and her weight is exactly where she most fears it being as a direct result of her eating behaviors (binges caused by excessive food restriction). Polly's main safety behavior is her attempt to follow extreme rules about acceptable foods. This gives her the feeling that her food intake is safe, but her resulting long-term problems include being anxious about her children's eating patterns, fear of loss of control over her own eating, and concerns about her own health. She is also missing out on many foods she used to enjoy.

In short, each of these three case examples reflects a person who started out trying to feel safer, but who ended up trapped by their safety behavior and feeling even worse (physically and mentally). In the same way, your own safety behaviors can have you trapped in your eating disorder, by stopping you both from eating healthily and from getting on with your life.

So what do you need to do to get out of the stranglehold that safety behaviors can have on you? First, you will need to understand that changing your behaviors is going to be key. This will need to be done gradually, so that you feel in control of yourself. However, it also means putting up with feelings of anxiety in the short term (i.e., you will be taking risks with your eating) in order to learn that eating normally does not have the effects that you feared (e.g., weight gain).

This is usually the point where sufferers think: "Maybe now is not the right time." So should you be thinking about change or not? If that is your first reaction, then it is time to go back to Chapters 5 and 6 of this book, in order to get clearer about what you are aiming to do.

Final tips on maximizing your chances of success

You are going to need to change in many ways and do lots of things to make this treatment work. Therefore, for it to work, you will need to put yourself first (see Section 2). This might be hard for you, as you might feel that you are being selfish or don't deserve this time and space. You deserve this just as much as anyone else, and things will not change if you do not prioritize your needs.

You might also read this book and think about skipping the bits that you do not feel comfortable doing. Many people would like to modify the program to make it easier to follow or to reduce their anxiety about change. You may be having some of the following thoughts:
- "I want to do all this apart from the bit about eating normally"
- "I will do all of it, but only if there is a guarantee that I won't gain any weight"
- "I would like to diet at the same time in order to lose some weight"
- "I want to get better without cutting down on my drug/alcohol use"

- "I think I eat regularly, and I'm not sure that the bits about eating regularly apply to me"
- "It all sounds fine apart from the bit about eating carbohydrates"

Unfortunately, planning to skip bits is just another safety behavior – it will make you feel calmer in the short term, but worse in the long term. See the section on the core elements of treatment (especially "therapy interfering behaviors" – below, p. 59) if you want to understand why these omissions are not going to help you.

What do I need to get started?

Go through this checklist. When you have ticked them all off, you will be in the best position to start treatment:

- Get a medical check-up. Tell your doctor that you are going to have a go at overcoming your eating problems, and ask them to check that you are medically fit. They might need to take blood (particularly for urea and electrolytes, liver function and full blood count), check your blood pressure and heart function, test your strength, or carry out other tests. Ask them to explain what these tests are for, so that you know what the point is.
- Get support. Talk to a best friend, partner, family member or other person. If you do not feel able to do this, then consider what self-help organizations exist. You need to make sure that others understand what you are doing and why. Without that understanding, they are less able to help.
- Make time for therapy. Clear an hour each week that you will always set aside for holding your own personal therapy session. In this session, you will need to be able to weigh yourself, look through your daily diaries, review your progress and plan your tasks for the next week. Put aside an amount of time (about an hour at the same time once per week), identify a place that is private and comfortable, and always make sure that you put in structure by having a written agenda, having your diaries to hand, etc.
- Get a treatment notebook. This notebook has two purposes. In the front, you will need to keep your food diary (see below for a template that you can use or photocopy). In the back, you will need to write down the skills and strategies that you learn as you read this book and as you change. The notebook will become your record of what works for you and what does not work – your personalized treatment book. Make the notebook one that you can carry round with you all the time. Over time the notebook will develop into your "relapse prevention" book – your essential tool to help make sure you don't slip back into your eating disorder.
- Get access to reliable weighing scales. Find somewhere where you can weigh yourself routinely, but no more than once a week. All scales weigh you slightly differently, in the same way that all clocks tell a slightly different time, so use the same ones each time.
- Devote the last page of your notebook to a list of your weights, taken at the weekly weighing. This is important because it means that you will be able to

find what your weight is actually doing and compare it to what you fear it is doing. Include a count of any other important behaviors, such as how often you vomit or binge, etc.

- Get some graph paper. Plotting your weight on a graph can make it easier to see the pattern of weight change over time.
- Work out your current body mass index (BMI). This is a measure of your weight as a proportion of your height, and is a much better indicator of your physical condition than your weight alone. The great majority of people will be healthiest if they are in the healthy range 20–25 (although this might be lower if you are from an Asian background, or higher if you are an athlete or male). If you are much below that range, then you are probably not going to be able to maintain that weight if you eat normally. If you are over that weight, then you will need to maintain it while treating the eating disorder – weight loss is only really achievable after you have got rid of the eating disorder (not before or during). Your BMI is worked out using the formula:

$$\text{BMI} = \frac{\text{your weight in kilograms}}{\text{your height in meters} \times \text{your height in meters}}$$

So, for example, if you weigh 63.4 kg and you are 1.76 m tall, then you have a BMI of 20.5 [63.4/(1.76 × 1.76)] – i.e., at the bottom of the normal range. In contrast, if you weigh 77kg at that height, then your BMI is 24.9 – at the top of the normal range.

With all this done, you are in a position to start changing and overcoming your eating disorder. The first element of such change is to have a plan – your personal blueprint for change.

The CBT plan for change

As we go through this CBT plan for change, use your therapy book to make notes of points that make sense for you.

How long will it take?

The time frame for your recovery will depend partly on your starting point. One key question is whether you are underweight or not. If you are in the normal range, then you might need to budget about 15–20 weeks of concentrated work to change both your lifestyle and your eating habits. This does not mean that you have to give up the rest of your life for the next 15–20 weeks – it is much better to learn these skills while you keep life going as much as possible. You will need longer if you are underweight. However, you might not be the best judge of whether you are underweight, normal weight or overweight, so take a minute now to work out your BMI (see above). If you are under a BMI of 18, then you might need about 30–40 weeks to learn all this and to add the weight that you will need in order to get back to health. If you are over a BMI of 30, then you probably need about 15–20 weeks to learn the basics and to normalize your eating, but you might need to allow for some years to slowly lose weight, if you want to (remember that word "slowly" – it is very important). Remember that these are only average times – some people will need more, some less. The most important thing is reaching the destination: not how long it takes you to get there. Some other things that might influence your recovery time frame include:

- Length of time you have had the eating problem
- Severity of bingeing
- Severity of purging
- Support from others

However, it is very important to remember that how much change you make in the early stages of your therapy will be critical. The more change that you make in your behaviors (and weight, if you are underweight) in the first one or two months, the better your chances of doing well overall. Giving yourself permission to delay starting change makes it more and more likely that you will never benefit, because all you will be doing is giving in to the safety behaviors (e.g., "It would be scary to eat snacks today, so I will start soon, but not now" becomes "I never did start eating snacks, and here I am where I started"). It is never too late to start, but the longer you take to do so, the more likely it is that you will feel like a failure, and the more helpless you are likely to feel.

What are the tasks and stages of getting better?

There are a whole set of tasks that you will need to undertake, and we will list them here before addressing each one in detail. However, the tasks do not come in neat "stages", as you will need to do all of these tasks at the same time sometimes, and you will need to return to earlier tasks sometimes. The tasks are:

- learning how your body works and how food is processed by the body
- understanding your individual eating disorder, and building a personal "road map" towards change
- understanding the CBT model and how to apply it to yourself
- carrying out the tasks of CBT that will help to change your thoughts, emotions, behaviors and physiology
- keeping in place the changes you have made (also called "relapse prevention")

Some basic facts you need to know: psychoeducation

Many people have slightly skewed ideas about food and its potential impact on their bodies. In addition, individuals with an eating disorder also tend to have distorted ideas about the impact of their eating behaviors, such as vomiting. The following (Table 8.1) is a list of topics that might apply to you and your eating disorder, tied to a series of appendices at the end of this book to give you the information that you are likely to need. We suggest that you go through the list (with a loved one if they are able to help you here) and try to work out how

Table 8.1

Key piece of information	Why do I need this information?	Where can I find this information in the book?
The effects of starvation/ restriction	To understand that many of the apparent features of your eating disorder might be caused by the effects of starvation, rather than showing that you are somehow damaged or deficient	Appendix 2 (contains a checklist so that you can see what effects you might be suffering, as well as a summary of the "Minnesota study")
Complications of anorexic behaviors	So that you are aware of the biological consequences of restriction/low weight (and that many of those effects are reversible if you regain weight)	Appendix 3
Complications of bulimia nervosa	So that you are aware of the biological consequences of behaviors such as bingeing and vomiting, and can discuss how to alleviate those effects with your physician	Appendix 4
Complications of specific bulimic behaviors	To ensure that you are aware of the impact of the specific bulimic behaviors that can have the greatest health risks (vomiting; laxative abuse; diuretic abuse; excessive exercise/overactivity)	Appendix 5 (vomiting), Appendix 6 (laxative abuse), Appendix 7 (diuretic abuse), Appendix 8 (exercise/ activity)
Does purging work?	To let you know that purging behaviors such as vomiting, laxative abuse and diuretic abuse are far less effective means of weight control than many people think, so that you can decide whether the limited (or non-existent) effects of these behaviors merit all the physical risks (see previous Appendices)	Appendix 9
Understanding weight change	To let you get a perspective on the difference between short- and long-term weight change, and how the behaviors that bring about short-term apparent weight change (e.g., taking laxatives) are not effective in helping you to maintain a stable weight	Appendix 10

The positive impact of eating regularly	To understand how having a regular pattern of eating can have biological and psychological benefits that can help you escape the eating problem	Appendix 11
Normalizing your food intake	To give you practical tips about how to get your eating more normalized (e.g., changing both structure and content), in a controlled manner	Appendix 12
Normal eating	To give you a general overview of how you can identify ways in which your eating is or is not normal.	Appendix 13
Food groups and what foods are in them	To help you identify foods that are in each group, to tell you what nutrients they contain, and to suggest quantities that will contribute to a balanced diet.	Appendix 14
The role of key (but feared) elements of healthy eating	To address the beliefs and fears that you might have about carbohydrates and fats in your diet, pointing out the essential role that each plays, so that you can see the potential benefits in changing your eating to include them in more balanced ways	Appendix 15 (carbohydrates), Appendix 16 (fats)

much these behaviors and beliefs relate to you as an individual. Then read the relevant appendix, and consider how its lessons might apply to you as an individual. One word of warning – many people use the internet to get this sort of information. We find that the information there is very variable in quality and sometimes contradictory. We suggest that you stick with the information here, or talk to a doctor, nurse or dietitian to get a clear picture of what you need to know to help you.

The aim of this "psychoeducational" material is to ensure that when you are considering the pros and cons of your eating behaviors and disorder and the possibilities of change, you are fully informed.

Building your own road map to recovery

To plan how you will get away from your own eating disorder, it is important to understand where you are, and how you got there.

Taking stock: where am I now, and how did I get here?

This exercise will help you start thinking about how you developed your eating disorder. To do it, we recommend that you open your notebook and jot down your answers to the following questions on a separate page:

- what is my weight and BMI? (You can work this out by using the information given earlier on page 52)
- how often have I used different behaviors this past week (bingeing, avoiding food, excessive exercise, vomiting, taking laxatives, checking my body)? Write down the frequency of all the ones that you have used
- what impact are my eating behaviors having on my life (physical, social, emotional, family, work)?
- what impact is my eating problem having on others (family, relationship, friends, children)?

This is where you are now – the start of your way out of the eating disorder trap. You should repeat this exercise on the same day every week while you are following this program, to see how you are getting on.

Now, let's think about the way in which your thoughts, emotions, physiology and behaviors interact to keep you trapped here. Please go back to Chapter 2, and remind yourself about that basic "hot cross bun" model underlying CBT – how those four elements all interact. Draw out a hot cross bun for yourself in your workbook, filling in the thoughts, behaviors, feelings and physical effects that apply to you. That might include thoughts such as "My weight will shoot up out of control," feelings like "scared" or "angry," behaviors such as "bingeing" or "vomiting," and physiological consequences such as feeling hungry, craving food, and having your mood worsened (see the starvation effects mentioned under the Minnesota study in Appendix 2). Make sure that your personal hot cross bun shows clearly how these elements are linked.

Where do I want to get to?

You have already thought (see Chapter 5) about your long-term goals when considering motivation (the five-year plan that you developed above), but it is also important to focus on the shorter-term goal of what you want to achieve by the end of therapy. Remember, just doing this therapy on its own will not get you to where you want to be in life, but on the other hand you are unlikely to achieve your longer-term goals if you do not engage in the therapy.

Whatever your long-term goals are, if you are going to get out of the eating problem long term, they will need to include the following four elements (mapping on to the hot cross bun):
• getting to and maintaining a manageable, biologically safe weight
• learning to overcome your bulimic behaviors (if you have any), and
• learning to accept your body as it is (i.e., not perfect)
• being happy with yourself, and less controlled by anxiety, anger, and depression
While the last three are generally desirable to most people, the first goal (getting to and maintaining a biologically safe weight) scares a lot of people who are trying to maintain a weight that is below normal. However, if you look at the hot cross bun model, you will see that it is not possible to get your emotions, thoughts, and behaviors straight if you are fighting against your body's biological needs. In short, for as long as you continue to ignore what your body needs, you will remain stuck in the eating disorder.

Put your personal set of goals for this therapy in your therapy book. Discuss them with your family and carers if that will help you see what is missing from life at present. You will need to come back to these goals when you get to the relapse prevention stage later on.

9

The practical steps of CBT for your eating disorder

Now that you have done the work outlined above, you are motivated, educated about the eating disorders, and have a clear set of goals. You are now ready to embark on the core tasks of cognitive behavioral therapy for your eating disorder. These include:

1. Developing and maintaining your motivation throughout your work towards recovery
2. Developing a regular, balanced pattern of eating to stabilize your weight (or increase it if your BMI is below 19–20) and to reduce your vulnerability to bingeing and purging
3. Identifying your beliefs about eating, shape, and weight and starting to test their accuracy
4. Resolving other issues that are important in the development and maintenance of your eating disorder (e.g., low self-esteem, perfectionism, interpersonal difficulties, negative body image)
5. Maintaining the changes that you have made in the longer term

Although these tasks will overlap, they will need to start in the order in which they are presented above. You are likely to be at Step 2 by about a week into treatment, so if you are not there after about two weeks, then go back to Step 1 and ask yourself what you are doing to stop therapy happening. Similarly, if you are not at Step 3 by about five to nine weeks into treatment, you need to review whether you are really doing the work outlined here. All of these steps should be documented in your treatment book. Review them at each personal therapy session, and write up your conclusions about yourself and about your eating, weight, and shape.

What if it is not working? Overcoming "therapy interfering behaviors"

One thing before starting on these therapy steps – think about your previous efforts to change. Are you likely to sabotage your chances of getting better? It seems pessimistic to think about potential problems so early on, but this is a common scenario across all steps and it is important to know what the roadblocks are before you meet them, so that you can plan your way around them (rather than working them out only after you have become stuck).

Such acts of self-sabotage in therapy are called "therapy interfering behaviors," because that is exactly what they do – get in the way of therapy. Sometimes they are intentional: more often they are not. What they all share is the capacity to throw your recovery off the rails. Some typical therapy interfering behaviors include:

- Not doing the core tasks, or not doing them consistently. These include making sure that you are physically safe (e.g., getting a check-up with your family doctor), recording what you eat on a daily basis, and weighing yourself once a week.
- Trying to lose weight while trying to overcome your eating disorder. Just remember, if you need to lose weight to get down to a healthy level, it is only going to work if you overcome your eating disorder first. When you try to lose weight during treatment for your eating disorder, you are putting yourself at risk of the treatment failing.
- Not taking the time for your personal therapy sessions – put them in your diary now, and make sure that you prioritize them. You might be very busy with your job, studies, family, etc., but you need to make sure that these all happen.

Now, go over that list (now and at every "personal therapy" session) and be honest with yourself – am I committed to therapy? If you are letting any of these tasks slip, then the answer is that you are not. That sounds harsh, but if you cannot be honest with yourself now, then you cannot get back on track to get back to normality and health. It is time to prioritize yourself and your health.

Step 1: Developing and maintaining your motivation

If you have read this far, then there is a good chance that you see yourself as committed to therapy. You will remember that we talked about this issue in Chapters 5 and 6. Now would be the perfect time to go back to those chapters and to the notes that you made about your own pros and cons, and the reasons why you have stayed stuck in the past (remembering your safety behaviors) as well as the short- and long-term reasons for changing now. However, let's be clear about the demands of therapy so that you know what you are committing to. First, this is going to take months rather than days or weeks. Second, it is going to occupy a sizeable chunk of your time, though it does not need to be something that occupies *all* of your time. Third, you will need to run routine "personal therapy" sessions with yourself – probably daily at first, then weekly. You need to ensure that you are available to do this. Your motivation to change will be an important topic to revisit whenever you are feeling stuck or scared of making the next change.

Step 2: Developing a regular, balanced pattern of eating

In order to develop a regular, balanced pattern of eating, the first thing to do is to be clear and precise about what you eat and drink. Then you need to be clear about whether changes towards a healthier pattern of eating will have the impact on your weight that you fear. Only when these basic things have been done will you be able to make sense of the therapeutic effects that a healthy eating pattern can have for you. Note that implementing this step will overlap with implementing Step 3, but you will need to start here.

Recording your eating

You should note down everything that you eat or drink every day. That includes times when you drink, binge, or just eat more than you planned. It also includes alcohol, as this can have a noticeable effect on your weight and eating behaviors (e.g., greatly increasing your risk of over-eating/bingeing). Recording all this will be hard at first, as you have to find the space to do it and overcome your emotional reactions to facing up to what you are eating. However, you will find it easier as it becomes more familiar and part of your daily routine. Appendix 17 gives you a diary sheet that you can photocopy and use daily, though you might want to change it to fit your symptoms (e.g., prepare a version that includes how much exercise you do, if that is relevant). Keep the diary sheets well organized and dated, so that you can look back on how far you have come as your therapy progresses.

You should fill the diary sheet in *at the time that you eat* (rather than at the end of the day or when you happen to have time) to ensure it is as accurate as possible. The aim of the diary is twofold. First, it will allow you to see how your eating relates to your weight, and to your thoughts, feelings, and behaviors. Second, it helps you to keep your brain "turned on" when you are eating, rather than allowing you to make decisions unconsciously ("on autopilot"). Without becoming aware of your unconscious patterns in this way, you will find it impossible to challenge your thinking and change your behaviors. As you become more aware, you can learn to eat in a planned, conscious, and healthy way. Later, this will allow you to progress to eating in an automatically healthy way. In other words, you will not need to keep a diary for the rest of your life, but you will need to do so for a number of months (rather than days) until you have resolved your eating disorder.

If you overeat and feel out of control, tick the "binge" column. If you make yourself sick, then tick the relevant column (or modify for other behaviors). Any time that you feel like bingeing or using vomiting/laxatives, put in a brief note about why in the "Comments" column. It helps if you can work out the reason before you do the behavior, as that will help you make your mind up about whether you want to or not. However, it may be that to begin with you are only able to think about this after the event.

Understanding how your eating is linked to your weight

Using the diary every day for several weeks will allow you to identify the true links between your eating and your weight. It is very likely that you believe that eating normally will make your weight shoot up uncontrollably, and that it is only by restricting your intake that you can possibly prevent this. The problem with this way of thinking is that you will be scared of eating normally, with the consequence that you can no longer test this belief to see if it is valid. As outlined earlier in this chapter, the probability is that your weight is like that of other people – it will remain stable or only go up slowly, even if you eat a lot more than your body needs (i.e., more than the 2000 kcal that a woman probably needs or the 2500 kcal that a man probably needs just to stay stable). The diary is to help you understand (over time) that the best predictor of your weight is what you eat – not how scared you feel or what your body feels like at the time.

To stress the value of the diary – it is only through the explicit combination of regular eating, monitoring that eating and weekly weighing that you can discover the real impact of eating on your weight and shape. Keeping the diary is a key element of treatment – without keeping the diary, you will not be able to benefit from this approach.

For sufferers who remain unconvinced as to the usefulness of diaries, we use the following analogy (Waller et al., 2007):

Imagine a shopkeeper whose shop is losing money. He must take some action – otherwise he is going to go bankrupt. He can do one of three things. First, he can rush around making lots of different changes, raising prices, discounting prices, sacking staff, hiring staff, in the hope that one of these will make the difference and his profits will improve. What might be the disadvantages – if any – of this strategy? If he adopts this strategy, he will probably be left feeling quite exhausted and rather helpless about his ability to change things. Can you see any similarities between this and your current approach to solving your eating disorder?

The second option is that he can sit down and think about what has worked in the past, what products have sold well, which staff have performed well. And he can make his changes according to this information. Can you think of any disadvantages of this strategy? It is certainly a better strategy than the first one, but there is a weakness in this plan of action. The shopkeeper is relying on his memory, and unfortunately the human memory is not infallible. All sorts of things can interfere with its functioning – lack of sleep, alcohol, emotions, or just time.

His third and last option is to keep detailed records, to identify the patterns of sales and losses, and to make his changes according to this. There are two advantages to this. First, it is the most accurate way of making decisions about change. Second, if the shopkeeper continues to keep records while implementing his changes, he will be able to evaluate accurately whether or not his changes are having the desired impact. How does this third strategy relate to the difficulties you're experiencing at the moment?

So treat keeping the diary as a critical part of your treatment. You will need to complete it regularly and promptly, so that you can learn from your experiences.

Weighing yourself

First, *before you get on the scales*, it is important to understand your body's weight. We have already talked about a healthy weight range, but it has to be remembered that:

- weight has a random element over the short term. However hard you might try to keep it stable, your weight will fluctuate from day to day and week to week (perhaps by as much as one to two kilos, owing to factors such as water retention around your period, what you last ate, when you last went to the toilet, what you are wearing, etc.). Many people with eating disorders try to "micromanage" their weight by keeping to a very rigid diet (e.g., same foods every time; identical number of kilocalories every day; weighing in the same clothes and at the same time of day), and then get disappointed when they realize that their weight still fluctuates despite their strenuous attempts to keep it stable. We find that it is best to consider your weight by taking an average weekly weight over the course of a month (i.e., four weekly readings), and only assume that your weight is really different if the average of the next four weeks is substantially higher or lower.
- what you eat (in the long term) is the only reasonably reliable predictor of changes in your weight. How you feel about your body, the fit of your clothes, etc. are very poor predictors. Very few people are able to detect weight changes with any reliability, whether they have an eating problem or not. We routinely ask patients what they believe has happened to their weight, and how they reach that conclusion, and their usual assumption is that their weight will have shot up (or stayed stable) even when what they have eaten is not enough to justify that conclusion. Given the random element of weight change in the short term (see above), their guess will be right at times, but just as wrong at other times.
- weight can go down as well as up. When reviewing your beliefs about your weight, it can be illuminating to ask yourself how often your weight has gone up vs. down. Many eating disorder sufferers are biased to assume that, for example, their weight has gone up on 75% of occasions. However, when reviewing their weight graph, they discover that their weight is actually going up on 25% of occasions, going down on 50% of occasions and remaining the same on the other 25% of occasions.
- it is important to contrast your beliefs about your weight with what is actually happening (see example below). When using the graph paper to keep a weight chart, use a black line to demonstrate what is actually happening to your weight, and a dotted line to show what you feel is happening to your weight. If you think that your weight has gone up by a kilo since your last weighing, then draw that in before you weigh yourself, using the dotted line. If you

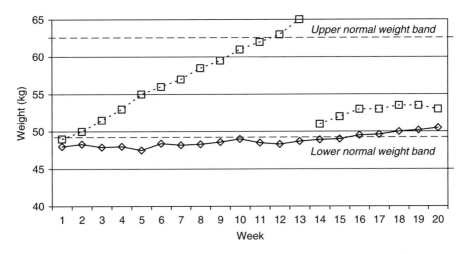

Fig. 9.1 Polly's weight chart (solid line shows actual weight: dotted line shows predicted weight changes).
Source: Adapted from Waller *et al.* (2007)

think that your weight has gone up by another kilo next week, then add that kilo to the dotted score from this week. If your beliefs are that your weight is shooting up, then you are likely to see a dotted line rocketing upwards, whether your actual weight is rising, falling or standing still (see Polly's graph, below). Weigh yourself on the same set of scales each time, as different sets of scales will give you different readings, adding to how difficult it is to be sure about your weight. Weighing yourself more than once a week will not be helpful, as all you will be able to measure is changes in fluid balance (changes in fat only occur over the longer term). This behavior can quickly become a safety behavior, offering you reassurance in the short term only. Because your weight will fluctuate randomly at different times of the day, weighing yourself lots of times is likely to maintain your anxiety about your weight going up ("Well, I was lighter half an hour ago than l was an hour ago and that felt like a relief, but maybe it will have gone up again so I had better check myself again").

A useful technique is to put your weight on a graph. That graph should show where your weight is now, relative to the normal range of BMI (20–25). If you have access to the internet, this can be done on many free websites.[1] The figure

---

[1] However, if you do not have access to a BMI calculator, then here is how to work out your "normal range" (i.e., a BMI of 20–25). To get your weight where you would have a BMI of 20, multiply your height in meters by 20, and then multiply that number by your height in meters again. This gives the weight (in kilograms) where you would be at the *bottom* of the normal weight range. To get your weight where you would be at a BMI of 25, then multiply your height in meters by 25, and then multiply that by your height in meters again. This is a healthy weight range for most people, though the lower limits might be a BMI of 19 in some cases (e.g., Asian women) and higher in others (e.g., athletes, males).

below shows Polly's weight chart, with her weight (solid line) spending most of the time just below a BMI of 20 ("Lower normal weight band"), and demonstrating how far her weight was from the BMI of 25 ("Upper normal weight band") that she was so scared of reaching. The dotted line demonstrates her weekly beliefs about her weight gain (see above), allowing her to see how her feared outcome (eating more normally leading to massive weight gain) did not materialize. Note that when Polly's predicted weight gain (dotted line) reached the top of the page, she simply started again from her current weight, Depending on your predictions, you may need to do the same.

Regular, healthy eating

However you eat now, it is time to start eating differently. The first step is to work towards a healthy *structure* of eating – beginning to move towards eating regularly, based on all major food groups (including appropriate levels of some carbohydrates and fats), whether you are underweight, normal weight or overweight. Use the healthy eating plan (below) to start organizing around a structure of three meals and three snacks per day, whatever you eat at each of those times.

The next step is to develop the *content* of what you eat – maintaining that regular pattern of eating and increasing amounts and diversity – either to help you avoid the need to binge, or (if you are underweight) to slowly gain weight to get to a safer place biologically. Many sufferers avoid specific foods (especially carbohydrates and fats) owing to their belief that eating those foods will result in immediate and significant weight gain. That belief can be a key target of CBT for the eating disorders.

Why can't you save eating differently until later? First, you have probably tried that in the past, and you know that it does not work. Second, we need to go back to that "hot cross bun" model (Chapter 2). The problem is that when people are deprived of core nutrition (particularly carbohydrates), it has a strong effect on their thoughts, feelings and behaviors. The lack of carbohydrate has the following impacts:

- Mood instability (e.g., becoming depressed very easily; anxious reactions; angry outbursts)
- Concrete, inflexible thinking (often described as being so focused on tiny details that one misses the big picture – "cannot see the wood for the trees"). This can involve obsessional rumination and checking, meaning that the individual has trouble in letting go of tasks, even if other things in life suffer.
- Cravings for food, leading to binges, hoarding food, using alcohol to get kilocalories, etc.

It is easy to see how these core problems will impact negatively on the sufferer's social life, relationships, family life, work, etc. Many people with eating disorders fear that this is part of who they are, so it can be a great relief to discover that one is not fundamentally "damaged" but having an understandable reaction to starvation and carbohydrate deprivation. Go back and read the section on the

Minnesota study (see Appendix 2) to get a clear picture of how food deprivation can affect people.

Putting it simply, would you expect anybody to be able to get out of their eating disorder if they had not dealt with those sorts of handicaps? Without improved eating, changes in your thoughts and feelings are particularly unlikely to happen. The desire to avoid working on your eating is a good example of a safety behavior – avoiding this key task will make you feel calmer at first, but will leave you trapped in your eating disorder in the long term.

The following analogy might be helpful. Imagine that you want to build a house. The original instructions say that you should start by laying the foundations, then build up the walls, then put the windows in, and so on. However, you really want to see what the view from the windows will be, so that you can feel motivated to do all the other work. So you start by putting the windows in place, but they fall down because there is nothing to support them. The original instructions are not random, but based on a logic that you will have to trust over and above your gut instincts. If you wonder whether this analogy applies to you, then think about the number of times that you have tried to "pull yourself together," or sworn that you were going to think or act differently tomorrow.

Just to stress this very important point – starting to leave your eating disorder behind means starting to change your eating towards a more normal and healthy pattern and content. So before you try to change your eating, you need to know what makes up normal eating. A normal healthy eating plan is detailed below.

A few practical tips to help you change your eating patterns

Some of the following might seem too obvious to believe that we are putting them down, but our experience with individuals with eating disorders has led us to recognize that it is always important to be willing to consider even such small possible changes. You might have a few of your own to add to the list:

- It can be helpful to plan your eating (e.g., the night before) to manage anxiety and ensure that you are not suddenly faced with having to make a decision about what to eat.
- Give yourself structure in the way that you eat and reduce distractions – pick one area where all you do is eat your meals and snacks (preferably at a table, but definitely not in front of the television), and then avoid eating in other areas of your home. It might feel strange at first, but give it a try – it really can work.
- Aiming to eat at regular times can reduce anxiety and help your body to relearn hunger and fullness.
- Make sure that you can get the food that you need when you need it (e.g., carry a cereal bar; buy a sandwich for eating later).

- If you are afraid that you will binge while you are out, start by taking only the minimum money that you will need for the day.
- Have structure when you are out shopping – prepare shopping lists; avoid "two for the price of one" offers if they might trigger a binge; avoid "danger zones" such as sweets and confectionery aisles.
- Do not shop while you are hungry.
- Make changes that are scary enough to have you worried, but not so scary that you never actually make them or you run away from them. If change is not scary, then it is unlikely to get your thinking patterns to change, so take small but meaningful steps.

Changing your eating pattern

Of course, this is the bit that most people find hardest – actually starting to change their eating pattern. You might not feel that you have much control over your eating, and the fear might be that changing to a healthier pattern will mean feeling that you have to give up on the little control that you do have. Staying stuck with your current eating pattern or trying to make inadequate changes (e.g., instead of eating no lunch, having a small salad instead) is not going to be enough. You need to think about just how far your eating is away from normal. For example, if your pattern is one of the following, then you will not be able to maintain it without being stuck in your eating disorder:

- "I try to avoid eating until the afternoon"
- "I try to get by on less than 1700 kilocalories per day"
- "I try to avoid all fat/carbohydrate"
- "I only eat fruit and salad if I can manage it"
- "I can get by without some meals"
- "I never snack"
- "I don't eat with others, for fear that they will think I am a pig"

Each of these ways of thinking (and many more) can result in inadequate eating and might mean that your body is deprived of core nutrition. They are also likely to result in the starvation features that underpin most eating disorders (see the section on psychoeducation, above, p. 53).

Changing the content of what you eat

The type of changes needed here vary hugely from person to person, because sufferers vary in what they are eating now. Here are some broad principles, underpinning the healthy eating plan that we will lay out below:

- Healthy eating involves a balance of foods, including carbohydrates, fats, protein, fruit, vegetables, etc. Any diet that takes out some of those elements is going to be unbalanced.
- A balanced diet will contain most of the vitamins and minerals that most people could need. Focus on the macronutrients (fat, carbohydrates, protein, etc.) and let the micronutrients take care of themselves.

- Many people with eating disorders tend to regard fat and carbohydrates as the enemy. This is to ignore the vital role of these nutrients in your body's maintenance, function, growth, and health
- Your body's main fuel source for day-to-day activity is carbohydrate. Complex carbohydrates (e.g., bread, potatoes, rice, pasta) will break down over a longer period of time, providing you with more sustained energy. Your body will respond to carbohydrate deprivation far faster than any other deficit. This is why your physical cravings can be so strong when you skip carbohydrate in your diet.
- Even the most complex of complex carbohydrates will run out after a few hours. This is why the healthy eating plan stresses topping up on food (in the form of meals and snacks) every three or four hours.
- A vegetarian diet is not a problem – you can be healthy following the same principles. While it is possible to achieve a healthy vegan diet (where no animal products are consumed, such as milk, cheese, honey), it is important to get your diet checked out by a professional (such as a dietitian – ask your family doctor for a referral), as it is possible that you will miss out on essential nutrients. It is also vital to ask yourself whether the decision to become vegan is in any way tied into your slide into developing an eating disorder. Was it a way of justifying cutting out all those foods, or was it a decision taken for other, more appropriate reasons?
- If you have a food intolerance, you will need to work around it. For example, if wheat is a problem (much less common than many people think), then use substitutes that supply complex carbohydrate.
- Fasting is a problem, whatever the reason. If you are expected to fast for religious reasons (e.g., Yom Kippur, Ramadan), then talk to your religious mentor about this, as most will tell you to treat your health as the priority (just as they would for diabetics).

If you are at a stable, normal weight (in the BMI range 20–25) at the start of the program, then if you undertake these changes it is likely that you will end up getting the same number of kilocalories that you are currently *absorbing* (but not as many as you are eating). However, this might mean eating far less, as you reduce both the amount that you binge on and the vomiting that gets rid of some (but not all) of that binge food. The key is to spread your fuel across the day.

If you are currently underweight (BMI <19–20), then you are going to need to eat more than you currently are during the phase of weight regain, but you will then have to reduce that amount again slightly (though probably not to your current level) when you have reached a normal weight, so that you can learn skills of weight stabilization. You might find that this comes quite naturally, as your appetite is likely to increase a little once you allow yourself a more appropriate diet (e.g., you really feel like a more substantial cereal bar/flapjack), but once your weight is at a healthier level your appetite reduces slightly (the flapjack seems less appealing compared to a banana or a smaller cereal bar).

Normal, healthy eating

Normal, healthy eating is something that varies from person to person and from cultural group to cultural group, but it is likely to involve the following:

- Eating about 2000 kilocalories if you are female or 2500 if you are male
- Eating a balance of carbohydrates, fats, proteins, fruit, and vegetables
- An adequate fluid intake (be guided by your body's level of thirst, rather than a regime)
- Some "fun" foods

Focusing on vitamins and minerals is probably unnecessary if your food intake and exposure to sunlight are adequate (unless you are pregnant or have a medical issue, in which case you should seek medical advice). The following gives a broad meal plan for keeping eating behaviors under control while maintaining a healthy weight (though if you are underweight then you will need additional food to help with weight gain):

Healthy eating plan

This plan is a simple menu guide (see Table 9.1 below) for one day, but can be used as a guide for eating over a longer period. It is important that you eat all the carbohydrate foods shown *in italics* (asterisks show where you can use the table section on the next page to find alternatives). Wholegrain and higher fiber types may satisfy hunger better.

The difference in amounts relates to people's differing energy needs. Over time, you will be better able to judge the amounts you need, but to start with you are advised to follow the plan fairly precisely.

Table 9.1 Healthy eating plan

Daily	200–300 mls (1/3 – ½ pint) of milk for teas and coffees
Breakfast	One glass fruit juice or one portion of fruit (e.g., apple, pear, small banana)
	/6 tablespoons of breakfast cereal (30 – 50g)* with milk/yoghurt/
	1–2 large slices of bread ** with butter/margarine and jam or similar
Mid morning	1 portion fresh fruit/2 plain biscuits (e.g., Rich Tea, Digestive), or similar
Lunch	*2–4 large slices of bread*
	** Meat/fish/cheese/pulses/beans/nuts/seeds or eggs
	Vegetables or salad
	Dessert – 1 carton of yoghurt (not diet) and a portion of fruit
Mid-afternoon	1 portion of fresh fruit/2 plain biscuits/a cereal bar/scone/teacake
Dinner	Meat/fish/cheese/pulses/beans/nuts/seeds or eggs
	2–4 large slices of bread**
	Vegetables or salad
	Dessert – see next table***
Supper	*1–2 slices of bread/crumpet/muffin* with butter/margarine or 2 plain biscuits, plus a milky drink

Table 9.2 Substitutions

Cereal*	6 tablespoons of breakfast cereal
	=30g/1oz of lighter cereals e.g., Rice Krispies/Special K, etc.
	=50g/2oz of heavier cereals e.g., muesli, Bran Flakes, etc.
	=2 Weetabix/Shredded Wheat
2 large slices of bread**	3 small slices of bread
	1 large/2 small bread rolls/1 bagel
	50–75g (2–3oz) rice, pasta, cous cous (dry weight)
	4–5 egg sized potatoes/3 small roast potatoes/18 small chips (fries)
	200–250g jacket potato
	2 scoops/3 heaped tablespoons mashed potato
	120g/4oz pizza
Dessert ideas***	Small slice of cake
	Small tin of rice pudding/individual dessert (not diet types)
	50g chocolate bar
	2 scoops ice cream

An adequate amount of fluid is between 1.5–2 litres (8–10 cups) drunk throughout the day. Lunch and evening meals may be interchanged, as may items themselves, although the format of the meals should remain as shown. The next table (Table 9.2) gives alternatives to the foods marked with 1–3 asterisks, and you can substitute the appropriate quantities as you wish. Aim for a variety of foods in your eating plan to help you achieve a balanced diet.

How can I get to normal, healthy eating from where I am now?

You need to take a close look at your current eating pattern relative to this normal, healthy eating pattern, and then work out how to make the change from where you are now to where you need to be. You need to make sure that your eating includes the two key elements outlined above – *structure* (a pattern of eating meals and snacks, with no gaps) and *content* (particularly, complex carbohydrates at all points).

As there are many ways in which your eating might differ from the healthy eating plan, it is not possible to be prescriptive here about how you should change your eating – that is your job. You have the start point and you have where you need to get to, so only you can work out the specifics of the route. However, here are some possible methods that might help:

- If you do not normally eat anything including complex carbohydrates until midday or the afternoon, then start by eating breakfast (as specified in the plan) and then gradually introduce the additional meals and snacks.
- If you eat meals only, then add in snacks as per the plan, but one at a time.
- Work gradually to reduce alcohol intake until it is within recommended limits, but if you are underweight then remember to replace the lost kilocalories with

ones from food (usually carbohydrates, as you might be drinking to replace missing carbohydrates in your diet). Check back over your diet diary to see which foods you are missing, and work on those.

• If you eat no complex carbohydrates, start by eating a small amount of complex carbohydrates at each meal and snack, and gradually increase to what is recommended.

• If you have had no set meal time, add one daily meal or snack (with carbohydrate content) each week until you are able to have three meals and two or three snacks per day. Start wherever you can in the day, but it is often best to start by adding in breakfast each day, then your mid-morning snack or lunch, and so on.

As you eat more along these lines, you need to be very careful that you are monitoring your weight. This is not necessarily because your weight will change dramatically, more because that is your fear, and getting evidence about the effect of eating more healthily/normally is a vital part of the work. You might take several weeks or months to move from your current eating pattern to a more normal one, using the steps outlined above, so keep a note in your diary over the weeks of how your eating structure and content are changing. When you have stabilized around a normal, healthy eating pattern, keep going for another four weeks, so that you can be clear what your average weight is under these conditions. It is now time to move on to the next step.

Summarizing what you have learned

As recommended earlier, you will also need to keep a record of your symptoms – a sheet in your notebook that records your progress on key features of your eating problem. At the end of each week, during a personal therapy session, add up how many times you did the following (as appropriate to your problem):

• ate a meal or snack (with the recommended complex carbohydrates)
• binged
• vomited or used laxatives (purged)
• used other behaviors (e.g., body-checked; exercised to lose weight)

And put in your weight, as taken at that session. This sheet will give you an overall picture of how your treatment is progressing. If you are in the normal weight range or above (your BMI=20+), then an important element of treatment will be getting rid of the bingeing and purging behaviors, while keeping your weight stable. If you are underweight, then an important part of change will be getting your weight to a stable and safe level (i.e., getting your weight up to a BMI in the normal range), as well as getting any such bingeing and purging behaviors under control.

Do the diary for one week without changing your eating pattern. This will give you a clear picture of what your eating is really like. In other words, you have begun to start the process of gathering evidence, outlined above. There will never be a perfect week to begin this (e.g., you will always be able to say, "But this week is not typical because"), so start now. And when you have recorded your intake for a week, it is time to move on to Step three.

Step 3: Challenging your thoughts and anxieties about weight

"Well, I changed my eating pattern so that I now eat to a much better structure, and things haven't gone wrong. However, there are still many things about my eating I am scared to change. How do I deal with these fears?"

As mentioned above, though this step will begin after Step 2, the two will run in parallel for a lot of your self-help treatment, as they facilitate each other. Therefore, do not be surprised if you find it helpful to flip between these sections.

Many of the thoughts we all have occur automatically. We experience a constant stream of thoughts, and if we attended to every single one then we would not achieve anything. The thoughts that we have on a regular basis do not necessarily need our full attention, so to free up space for us to attend to new information, these regular thoughts slip below the level of our conscious awareness (i.e., you will not necessarily notice them unless you make a conscious decision to do so). Therefore, a lot of our routine behaviors (e.g., eating) are more influenced by these automatic thoughts than by active/conscious thinking. These automatic thoughts have developed over many years, and as a result the way you see the world is determined more by these automatic thoughts than the way things actually are. When such automatic thought patterns become a problem, they are known as "dysfunctional assumptions."

Challenging your thoughts

Before you apply this way of thinking to your eating and weight, maybe it is time to try out an exercise or two in challenging your beliefs in other parts of your life. What this involves depends on your own life, but here is an example:

- Belief: "The bus is never on time. Maybe one time in ten it gets here on time, but not the rest of the time".
- Alternative belief: "Maybe the bus comes on time more often than that, but I am always worried about getting to work late so I am worried that it will be late".
- Ways of developing evidence: "I could keep a record of how often the bus comes on time – say within 5 minutes of the scheduled time – and how often it does not".
- Outcome: "Well, looking at my diary, the bus comes on time about 60% of the time. Therefore, my original belief was wrong, but now I know that, I can adjust when I get to the bus stop to ensure that I am on time when I have to be at work dead on time."

This way of approaching your thought processes will be very important to your recovery, as you will need to re-evaluate so many elements of your behavior around your eating, shape, and weight. Remember, while it is scary to consider behavior change, without doing so it is very unlikely that anything is going to change.

Now think about how you can challenge your thoughts about eating. First, go back to the "hot cross bun" diagram in Chapter 2 (Fig. 2.1). It is easy to see how having those dysfunctional ways of thinking could have a strong effect on your feelings. For example, if you strongly believe that your weight is going to shoot up, then of course you feel anxious, and maybe angry that others do not understand. In the context of having that thought and emotions, it makes sense that you will try to restrict your intake. The difficulty for other people in understanding your feelings and behaviors is that they do not have the same assumptions about what will happen to you if you eat.

Therefore, a key element in therapy for your eating disorder is going to be learning to challenge this automatic way of thinking. This means that you will have to learn to identify such thoughts, and then challenge them. This involves weighing up the evidence for those beliefs and for the alternatives. Such evidence might already exist, or you might need to work out a way of generating it. "Thought challenging" is a way of exploring other ways of thinking about things, commonly through making predictions about what will happen if you change your safety behaviors and try something different.

For example, remember the case of Katy (Chapter 1), who was trying to control her weight through missing meals and snacks and by exercising. Her assumptions were that her weight would accelerate out of control if she did not restrict her food. For example, she had beliefs such as: "If I eat anything before mid-afternoon, I will lose control and binge." Such thoughts made her both very anxious (emotion) and avoidant of food (behavior). The food avoidance then had the knock-on effect of making her starve, resulting in binges, and the thought was: "I have to restrict my food more because I binged yesterday." Alternative thoughts might be: "If I eat in a regular way, starting early in the day, then I will be less likely to binge because I will not be making my body crave carbohydrates" and "I binged because I starved, so to starve myself after I binge is likely to result in another binge."

To compare these beliefs it might be possible to compare days in the past when you have eaten in one pattern versus the other, to see which pattern is more associated with binge-eating. However, it might be the case that you have been stuck in this pattern for so long that you cannot make such comparisons from recent experience. In such circumstances, the most effective way of finding out which way of thinking is more appropriate will be to try out both patterns of behavior and see which one is associated with binge-eating.

There are a number of useful tools for helping you to identify and challenge your thoughts:

Thought records. Because thoughts are so often automatic, you might find that your behaviors and your emotions have been triggered and you have no idea why. This is very common, and quite normal (see above regarding the automatic nature of many thoughts). However, if your thoughts are problematic ones, then it is necessary to identify them so that you can challenge them consciously. Keeping a written record of your thoughts, emotions, and behaviors will bring them into your conscious awareness, so that challenging becomes possible. Very often, the trigger for completing this will be when you use a particular behavior (e.g., bingeing, vomiting, missing a meal, weighing yourself) or experience a change in your emotions (e.g., sudden feeling of panic), as such behaviors and emotional switches are more easily identified than automatic thoughts. So, when you notice either a particular behavior or a sudden change in your emotions:

1. Record this in your diary (the sooner you record this the more accurate your account will be).
2. Record the situation/context.
3. Record the emotion/behavior (whichever is missing). Remember if you are recording an emotion you should be using single words (e.g., panic, sad, angry). If you are using sentences or phrases, then you are more likely to be recording the context of your thoughts.
4. Finally, try to identify the thought that might have triggered the emotion and the behavior that followed. To begin with you might have to guess at what this might have been, but you are the best person to do this and with practice will be able to work out whether these guesses are accurate.

As a result of writing down as much as you can about the situation/context (e.g., "When I binged, I was on my own, just after a phone call from my father where he told me off, and I had not eaten all day"), you can consider what the thoughts and feelings might have been that triggered the behavior (e.g., "I was feeling angry at him for telling me off, and thinking that I wish I could just tell him to leave me alone at times, when I feel I am doing OK – he always knocks my self-esteem down when I feel happy"). Armed with these links between thoughts, feelings, and behaviors, you can start to write down alternative and more healthy ways of thinking about and coping with this pattern, where you do not need to use food (e.g., "If it is him calling, I am going to screen my calls and not answer. Then I will have something to eat, wait until it has gone down, write down a few thoughts about why I think he is so bossy and critical, think of some positive things that I can tell him to make myself feel positive without upsetting him, so that he can't upset me").

Table 9.3 is an example of a "thought record" that Polly completed whenever she found herself avoiding foods on the grounds of their being "unhealthy," allowing her to consider the validity of the thoughts and emotions that underpinned her avoidant behaviour. Appendix 18 gives you a blank thought record sheet to help you do these challenges as you progress. Note that the columns are in the order outlined above, as it can be helpful to start by noticing the behavior and then working from there. You will normally find it easiest to progress from the left-hand column to the right-hand one, but you are unlikely to be able to complete all the columns until you have practiced the first few and got good at them. If you cannot work out what you might have been feeling or thinking, then you might ask your loved ones to help you out when it comes to thinking what might belong in each column.

"Every time I find myself making the 'healthy' choice (i.e., deliberately avoiding fats and carbohydrates)"

Table 9.3 Polly's thought record sheet

Date/Time	What did I do?	What was going on at the time (context)?	What was I feeling that made me act that way?	What thoughts was I having that made me feel and act that way?	What alternative way of thinking about that situation might have been more helpful?	What might have been a better way of dealing with that situation?
Tuesday lunch time	Without thinking about it, I chose "safe" foods for myself and for the children.	I was getting lunch for myself and the children, and I looked at the table and realized that I had chosen only low-calorie foods, like salad and crispbread, with no spreads or anything else.	I think I must have been *anxious* about what would happen to my weight, and whether I would have a reaction to the foods that I know the children would like (and that I like if I let myself have them).	"I am going to put on lots of weight. Eating those 'forbidden' foods will make my stomach swell up hugely and I will feel bloated and ugly."	"All I have learned about these foods suggests that they will not have this effect. However, because I am anxious, I will feel bad for a bit, but that will fade as I tolerate it."	To try adding in new foods that are on my "forbidden" list and that I know the children will like, put up with my anxiety, and see if there is any real change in my body or how I feel.

Positive data logs. Everybody makes errors when they process information about the world. Most people tend to make positive errors, overestimating their own responsibility for positive things happening, and underestimating how responsible they are for negative things. People with an eating disorder have the opposite pattern of thinking, tending to be very self-critical and underestimating their ability to cope. As well as challenging automatic thoughts about food it is important that you find positives about yourself and about how you can cope in the world. In order to build self-esteem, we suggest that you keep "positive data logs" to help you correct such information-processing errors, allowing you to see the positives in how you cope. Write down a list of the positive things that you and others can identify about yourself. This will mean spending time focusing on your achievements (e.g., qualifications, relationships, friendships, children), ways in which you have coped successfully in a range of settings (e.g., succeeding at work, even though there are many pressures), and your journey towards potential positive events (e.g., promotion, etc.). Having these positives summarized (and adding to the list as you proceed to change) can be invaluable in helping you to challenge the cognitions (thoughts) that are holding you back. This needs to be an ongoing process, and you will need to spend time to get better at noting the positive bits about yourself, so take five minutes at the end of each day to highlight and record achievements, however small (e.g., managing to get out of bed when you really didn't feel like it). Add them to your list, in order to counterbalance your tendency to criticize yourself or underestimate your ability.

Flashcards. A flashcard is a quick and effective way of reminding yourself about key lessons. When you have spent time planning how to cope with particular situations (e.g., following using thought records to make your negative thought processes clearer and developing challenges to your negative automatic thoughts) or when you have developed a list of positive aspects about yourself (e.g., using your positive data logs), then the flashcard is a quick and effective way of reminding yourself about those conclusions and action plans when you most need it – when there is a problem. If you know that a particular issue is likely to come up (e.g., feeling anxious about eating carbohydrates), then write a brief note to yourself in advance about what you have learned so far, what your automatic reaction is likely to be, and what you could do instead (e.g., "When I am panicky about eating carbohydrates, I should remember that there is no evidence that I swell up when I eat them; my anxiety is caused by my automatic thoughts, rather than by what is actually happening; if I eat carbohydrates then my mood is calmer in the long run, and I know that I function better at work and when I get home"). This note is often put on an index card, to allow you fast access to an alternative way of thinking – hence the term "flashcard." You can have as many of these as you like, as long as you can access them as and when you need them. Some of our patients have found it useful to keep them on their mobile phone, or as a screen saver on their computer, or have kept their index card in their wallet. By preparing these flashcards in advance, you can be sure that healthy alternative ways of coping are at your finger tips, rather than hoping that you will be able to access these from memory (a tricky thing for anyone to do when they are feeling overwhelmed by strong emotions or in the middle of what feels like a crisis).

Continuum thinking. An important skill is to learn to reduce black-and-white/all-or-nothing thinking (e.g., "If I put on any weight at all, it will be a disaster"; "I have no redeeming features at all"; "I am always the fattest person in the room"). Reducing this type of thinking will lead to a more balanced and calm way of looking at the world, resulting in less extreme and overwhelming emotions. If you are restricting your food intake, you might notice that you are particularly prone to thinking in this way, as starvation can make it even harder to think in shades of gray. If you find that you tend to think in a black-and-white way (e.g., "Either I am not hungry at all or I am ravenous"), then it can be useful to try looking for finer distinctions between your thoughts (e.g., keeping a record of how hungry you are on a 0–10 scale, until you can perceive that you can be anywhere between not hungry and ravenous, rather than at one end or the other).

This type of thinking becomes harder to shift if you link unrelated concepts in a black-and-white way (e.g., "Only thin people are attractive"; linking size [concept 1] with attractiveness [concept 2]; "Only thin women get boyfriends" linking size [concept 1] with relationships [concept 2]). If you do this, then it can be helpful to start examining the validity of the links between the concepts. The following illustrates a way in which you can do this if you believe: "Only thin people are successful people."

- *Step 1:* Write down the current belief and rate its strength ("Only thin people are successful people" – 90% certain).
- *Step 2:* Write down the names of ten people who you know (friends, family or acquaintances, but not yourself).
- *Step 3:* Draw a line, with one end of the line marked "Thinnest" and the other end marked with a term that means the opposite for you (e.g., "Fattest"), and place the ten people, using their initials, at the appropriate places on that "continuum" line (starting by putting the thinnest and fattest of the ten people at the extreme points on the line [see] Step 3, Figure 9.2).
- *Step 4:* On a fresh sheet of paper, repeat Step 3, but with the continuum line marked "Most successful" to "Least successful" (or whatever makes sense for you). Our patients find this takes some time as they realize success can be defined across a range of areas such as work, family, hobbies, and friends. You now have two continuums, based on the same ten people (see Step 4, Figure 9.2).
- *Step 5:* Reframe the current belief as a diagram, with the two continuum lines at right angles see (Figure 9.2). If your belief is right, then everyone should fall along (or very near, given that the prediction is 90% certain) the line going at 45 degrees to the other lines – in other words, thin people will be successful, fatter people will be less successful, and everyone else will fall along the line accordingly (i.e., within the curved lines). Ask what it would say about your belief if these people did not neatly fit this pattern (generating your alternative belief), and how strongly you believe in that alternative (usually a very low rating).

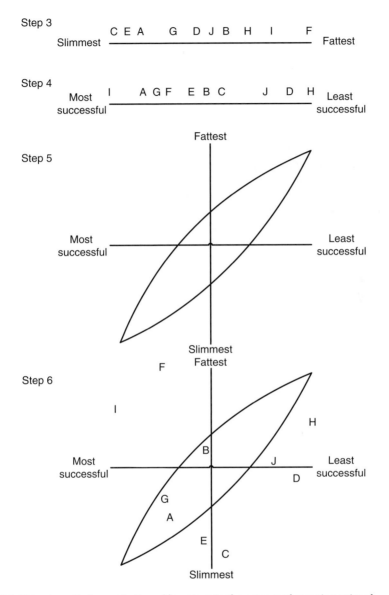

Fig. 9.2 Diagrammatic demonstration of key steps in the process of mapping pairs of continuum lines to test out the belief "Thinner people are always more successful" (each letter refers to one person).

Source: Adapted from Waller *et al.* (2007)

- *Step 6:* Now it is time to test the accuracy of your current belief. Start putting the people into the diagram, according to where they belong on each of the individual continuum lines. Our experience is that the individuals whom you have chosen show up scattered around the graph, rather than on the prediction line or within the curved lines (ellipse), as is the case here (see diagram). It is time to think "What might be going on here?"

- *Step 7:* It is time to re-rate the strength of your belief (and the alternative), and to try to reframe it (e.g., "Did I have the right attribute/quality to associate with thinness?"; "Did I pick the wrong ten people?"). You might conclude that the importance of thinness must be that it is associated with a different attribute or quality to the one that you originally chose (e.g., attractiveness rather than success). That possibility takes you to the next step.
- *Step 8:* Repeat this exercise, in order to see if you can work out what attributes are reliably associated with thinness, etc.
- *Step 9:* Consider the possibility that the "thinness results in attribute x" belief does not work, and that it might be more important to understand what else might help you achieve "attribute x" (e.g., control, happiness, friendships) if thinness is not the answer. This pattern of thinking can lead you to consider other possible ways of achieving attribute x, rather than dieting, etc.

This method of thought challenging can create a good foundation for more powerful ways of changing your thinking patterns (e.g., behavioral experiments – see below), as it can open your mind up to the possibility of alternative ways of looking at the world. In turn, such ways of thinking will make you feel more confident about taking the risk and trying something new.

The next step. A more evidence-based way of thinking is something that will be needed throughout your treatment. Now that you are aware of its importance, it is time to start generating some of that evidence. The first step in generating alternatives to your automatic ways of thinking is to start recording what you have actually eaten, so that you can learn whether this is a better way of explaining your weight than your fears that it will shoot up in an uncontrollable way. Time to move to the next step, but remember to come back here whenever you feel yourself getting stuck with your thoughts and your behaviors.

Changing your eating: exposure

The next element of change is based on the principle of "exposure." This involves putting yourself in a scary situation (e.g., eating carbohydrates), and coping with the anxiety that this situation causes. That means staying with the anxiety until it fades naturally, which it does because of physiological actions (your body cannot stay in such a heightened state of arousal for long – about 30–40 minutes is usually the maximum for a single reaction), but your anxiety will need longer, as the thing you are afraid of keeps coming back in the form of meals, snacks, etc.). Throughout, you will need to stay with the anxiety rather than engaging in the common reaction of reducing the anxiety through using a safety behavior (e.g., vomiting; changing back to a "safer" way of eating).

It is normal for your body to react to anxiety with an urge either to fight the thing that is scaring you or to run away from it – commonly called a "fight or flight" reaction. However, while that reaction is helpful where the object of your anxiety is a real threat (e.g., a mugger threatening you), it is not helpful where the object of the anxiety is not a real threat. The problem that many people have is that they assume that non-threatening objects and events are dangerous (e.g., being scared of spiders), and hence run away before they can learn that the anxiety fades and they can conclude that there was no real reason to be afraid.

In the case of eating more normally, you are aiming to build your confidence in the fact that the thing you fear (e.g., uncontrolled weight gain) doesn't happen. However, becoming confident that your fears are not going to be realized takes time, so you will need to persevere with regular eating (no safety behaviors) for a while, tolerating the anxiety that this will undoubtedly trigger. Eventually your weight graph will help you see that your weight is staying stable (i.e., within a range of about 2 kg), and your anxiety will drop and your confidence rise. Section 2 gives you some strategies for managing emotional states, including anxiety, so re-read those strategies as you try out eating more normally.

After you have been exposing yourself to your fears for four to eight weeks, you should be starting to feel a bit more confident that what you fear is not going to happen. Now, it is time to push harder. Instead of exposure, you move on to behavioral experiments.

Systematically changing your eating: behavioral experiments

A behavioral experiment is like exposure, but is a better challenge of your beliefs because you are encouraged to be very clear about what you will do differently (e.g., eating a specific extra amount of a feared food), and to use that change to challenge your beliefs about the specific results of that change. You are seeking evidence that your existing beliefs are correct (e.g., "If I start eating breakfast every day, my weight will shoot up by 3 kg in a month and I will binge more") or that alternative beliefs are more accurate (e.g., "If I eat breakfast every day, then my weight will stay stable or even fall and I will binge less"). As with any experiment, the more that you can keep everything else the same, the clearer you can be about what you have learned (e.g., "but all this will only tell me anything if I do not increase my exercise or cut out other meals to compensate for the changes").

Behavioral experiments are a challenging but powerful way of changing your fears about your eating, weight, and shape – thus freeing you up to eat normally again. They allow you to gather concrete evidence to evaluate the accuracy of your automatic thoughts. The important thing is to treat both your existing belief (e.g., "My weight is going to shoot up and I will binge more if I start to eat regularly") and the alternative belief (e.g., "I might be eating more regularly, but that will help me not to binge so I will probably take in no more food overall, and therefore my weight will stay the same") as possibly accurate, and to stick with the behavioral change long enough to be able to reach conclusions. Just remember that this is about testing your beliefs, and that using your safety behaviors (giving up the experiment because it makes you anxious about gaining weight) will keep you stuck in your eating disorder.

Appendix 19 is a sheet that allows you to plan out a behavioral experiment for yourself. The following example will give you an idea of how to do that. The steps are as follows:

1. First, you need to consider the thoughts about food, shape, and weight that keep you scared and stuck in your eating disorder. These might be something like: "Eating bread will make me put on loads of weight." The next step is to make that thought into a concrete prediction, such as: "If I eat four slices of bread per day, then I will put on at least one kilogram in a week." The accuracy of that sort of belief can be tested because it is very specific. Then you should rate how certain you are about that belief, on a 0–100 scale: "I am 95% certain about that."

2. Next, you need to consider an alternative belief, possibly based on your reading of the psychoeducation material in this book, or from talking to other people. This belief needs to be one that you can compare directly with your current belief, such as the following: "Eating four slices of bread per day, I should only be able to put on about a quarter of a kilogram in a week." That belief also needs a certainty rating: "I think that is only 5% likely."

3. Now that you have your two beliefs, you need to work out a way of comparing them. In this case, you would need to eat four slices of bread a day, so that you can find out which prediction is more accurate. If you find that too scary to try, then you need to reduce the level of change and adjust the beliefs accordingly (e.g., "If I ate half a slice of bread per day, I would still be scared that my weight would go up by a kilogram in a month, but I think I could manage that"), but remember that you will need to make enough change to make you anxious, so don't reduce the amount of change to a level where you get comfortable. It is really important not to change anything else about your eating at the same time, as that will stop you being able to make sense of the outcome later on.

4. Once you have your contrasting beliefs and you have worked out how to compare them, the next thing to do is to decide how long you need to run the experiment. Remember that weight fluctuates, so any change in weight over a single week is unlikely to be meaningful. Usually, four weeks is a good time frame for making meaningful change – compare your weight over the four weeks post-change with the four weeks before the change.

5. Now make the change in your behavior. Make sure that you can do what you need to (e.g., having enough bread available; weighing yourself), and remember that your anxiety is a normal and necessary part of the process rather than a problem.

6. At the end of each week, make sure you have recorded all the necessary information on your worksheet. If there were any difficulties (e.g., you did not do the experiment on one day), plan ahead to ensure this does not happen again. Remember, do not make any judgements until you have completed all four weeks.

7. At the end of the four weeks, re-evaluate your beliefs. What was your average weight over the four weeks before you changed your behavior? What has

happened over the four weeks of the experiment? Which of your two beliefs was closer to what actually happened? How strongly do you hold the two beliefs now?

8. Use what you discovered in this experiment to help you to plan the next. With each experiment you will find that you are more accurately able to assess the validity of your beliefs about eating, shape, and weight.

Behavioral experiments can be used to test out a whole range of beliefs that could be keeping you stuck in your eating disorder. For example:

- "If I eat snacks, then I will binge." *Experiment:* Start by keeping a count of how many times a week you binge at present, then add snacks to your diet, and see if the existing beliefs are right (i.e., you binge more) or if the alternative belief is more accurate (i.e., you binge less).

- "I have to keep weighing myself several times a day, because my weight will shoot up if I don't." *Experiment:* Look at your weight on your chart, and draw out what you think will happen to it over the next few weeks if you do only check your weight weekly. Then try not weighing yourself more than once a week, and see if your weight changes as you predicted (original belief) or if it stays stable (alternative belief).

- "I can't eat in front of other people, because they will comment on my weight or otherwise criticize me." *Experiment:* Predict what people will say, focusing on your beliefs about being criticized (i.e., comments that are hostile, rather than positive or neutral). Try eating with others, and see if you are correct, or not.

Behavioral experiments can be fairly short, but might need to go on for several months in a planned way. You will need to continue the experiment until you feel you have enough evidence to assess the accuracy of both thoughts properly (your current thought and the alternative).

The following is an example of a behavioral experiment carried out by Jenny in trying to overcome her anorexia nervosa. In order to try to increase her weight, she planned to add in a cereal bar as each morning's snack. She planned out the experiment using the template in Appendix 19. On this occasion, Jenny's fear was not that her weight would go out of control because of eating the cereal bar, but that she would begin to binge because of breaking her "eat no snacks" rule, and that her weight would go up because of the binges. Jenny was very certain that this would be the result, and very certain that the alternative belief (that she would not binge) would be proven to be wrong. She decided that she would need four weeks for her existing thinking to be proven right or wrong, and that she would have to keep her other eating stable and not exercise more to compensate for the extra cereal bar. To test out her beliefs, Jenny began by preparing a chart like the one below, with the headings and the first two columns filled in. Each week, she prepared a summary of the week's developments, using her food diaries, including whether or not she had stuck to the plan. She then reviewed the outcome of the change in her behavior, and reviewed the strength of her initial belief and the alternative that she had developed. This let her complete the remaining columns of the chart in Table 9.4.

Table 9.4

Week	Behavioral change (every day)	What happened when I tried the change? (review at the end of the week, using my diary)	Initial belief to test ("I will binge daily if I have this snack")	Alternative belief to test ("I will not binge if I have this snack")
1	Have a cereal bar as a mid-morning snack	Binged on one day, but I realized that I had taken out lunch that day, so not sure what to make of that	100%	0%
2	Have a cereal bar as a mid-morning snack	Planned, had the mid-morning snack and had my usual lunch. Strong urge to binge on some days but I didn't!	80%	10%
3	Have a cereal bar as a mid-morning snack	Kept my eating as it was last week. Felt less guilty. Less worried about weight than I expected.	50%	20%
4	Have a cereal bar as a mid-morning snack	Kept on doing the task. Went OK again – no binges and my weight has not changed for this whole month. I can't believe this! I want to know if I can push it a bit further in the next experiment. Looks like I will have to eat more if I want to get my weight to go up, but at least I am not so terrified of starting to binge if I make more changes to my eating.	40%	60%

Following these changes in her behavior and her beliefs, Jenny was eager to try further change, as she came to realize that the weight gain that she needed to achieve was going to require eating a lot more than she had tried out up to that point.

After your work so far on eating normally, cognitive (thought) challenges, exposure and behavioral experiments, it is time to think: "Has this helped?" Sometimes, changes in our attitudes can be so slow that they are difficult to detect.

Table 9.5 Questionnaire 1b : Do I have a problem with my eating?

Just tick the answer that most closely describes your feelings or actions on each of these points	Not at all	A little	Sometimes	Most of the time	All of the time
I spend time worrying about whether I have put on weight					
I worry that my body will get bigger if I don't keep my eating very tightly controlled					
I have to restrict what I eat and/or exercise in order to compensate for the fact that I have eaten too much					
I take laxatives and/or make myself sick to help control my weight and size					
My eating pattern means that I cannot live the life that I want to					
I spend a lot of time checking my weight, measuring myself, checking my reflection, etc.					
I feel ashamed of my eating pattern					
My eating distresses those around me (my family, friends, etc.)					
My health suffers as a result of my eating					
My relationships are limited because I have an eating problem					
I eat because I am upset, rather than because I am hungry					
Controlling what I eat is more important than any other element of my life					
I exercise a lot, even if I am injured or it gets in the way of socializing with my friends (professional athletes excepted)					

However, no matter how slow the change is, it is important to stop and acknowledge it. This is an important part of building your confidence in your ability to change and your motivation to continue doing so. So, this may be a good time to complete the questionnaire (see Table 9.5) that you filled out in Chapter 1 again.

Now, go back and see whether the answers that you have given here are different to those given in Chapter 1. You should hopefully notice that the scores should have shifted (to the left). Put that in your positive data log (see above), to remind you of the benefits of your hard work.

Step 4: Addressing negative thoughts and feelings about your body

How you feel about your body might still be preoccupying you. Many individuals with eating difficulties will experience body dissatisfaction, though this does not apply to everyone. Such dissatisfaction can affect many aspects of your life, such as your self-esteem, mood and behavior (e.g., avoiding certain situations; only wearing certain types of clothing, not feeling comfortable with your partner seeing or touching your body). It is often the last element of eating concerns to be resolved, so do not worry if you have managed to address your eating but are still experiencing body-image dissatisfaction – this is very normal. We find that through the use of some of the strategies outlined below these negative thoughts and feelings can gradually be reduced.

It is important to remember that the goal when working to improve your body image is one of *acceptance* rather than complete satisfaction. Total body satisfaction is relatively rare among young women in particular (although men are also vulnerable to body dissatisfaction). Most healthy individuals are accepting of their bodies, rather than feeling totally satisfied with them (i.e., they like some bits, dislike other bits, but at the end of the day it is just their body – not something that has the power to influence every thought they have or every decision they make). To get to the point where you accept your appearance can take a considerable amount of time (months, rather than days and weeks), so you will need to allow yourself this time.

What is body image?

Put simply, body image is about the relationship we have with our bodies. Our body image might or might not be accurate or correspond with what we actually look like. Body image has a number of components:
- Perceptual/physical: what we see when we look at our bodies (including our errors, such as the very common error of seeing ourselves as bigger than we actually are).
- Cognitive: our intellectual judgements of our bodies.
- Emotional: what we feel when we look at or think about our bodies.
- Behavioral: what we do when we look at our bodies, and what we do that maintains our body image.

These components all come together to influence how we interact with our bodies, as shown in the CBT "hot cross bun" (Figure 9.3).

For example, when Katy sat down she noticed how her thighs spread on the chair (perceptual/physical). She thought: "My thighs look disgusting, I'm sure that other people look at me and see only cellulite" (cognitive), she felt anxious and sad (emotional), and she began to body-check (behavioral). Using the hot cross bun model, we can see how these factors all interact and become self-maintaining (e.g., Katy's body-checking made her calmer in the short term, but more anxious and depressed in the longer term by focusing her attention [thoughts] on the aspects of her body she liked the least).

How did my body image develop?

Body image develops from an early age. Puberty, with its rapid associated physical changes, often causes us to focus more on our appearance. There are two broad influences on body image – individual experiences and influences,

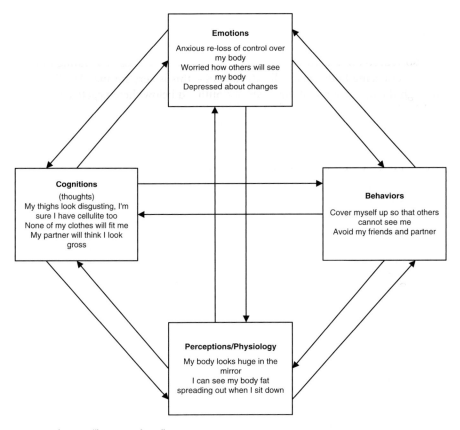

Fig. 9.3 The CBT "hot cross bun."

and cultural factors. The following *experiences* can be important in understanding the development of your body image:

- being teased and bullied (particularly if this focused on appearance in some way)
- being tall or reaching puberty early
- feeling in some way different (e.g., having to wear glasses from an early age)
- having a parent, friend or partner who placed an emphasis on looks
- having been abused (whether emotional, sexual or physical)
- receiving negative or positive comments about shape or appearance
- early experiences of being overweight or having family members who were overweight

Sometimes, interests or hobbies that require a certain shape (e.g., gymnastics, ballet) can also focus our attention on our body image.

Cultural factors vary across time and location. For example, in some countries there is value attached to pale skin, while in others a tan is seen as desirable. The ideal body size and shape also vary with fashion and across time. Such factors contribute to the idea that in order to be happy or successful, we need to look a certain way.

What maintains my body image?

As well as these historical influences, there will also be current influences that serve to maintain your body image, sometimes overlapping with the developing factors. These current influences include messages that you receive from others (friends, partners, relatives, the media), as well as your own thoughts about your body. You may also be engaging in behaviors that reinforce your thought by focusing your attention on the bits you like the least (e.g., comparing yourself to others, always wearing baggy clothing, spending lots of time and money on your appearance in an attempt to look "good enough") and away from other aspects of yourself (e.g., parts of your body that you think are OK, such as your hair or eyes, or your personality/character – such as being caring, funny, and intelligent).

Use your notebook to think about how your own body image might have developed. Jot down the early experiences that might have led you to focus on your body in a particular way. Now think about the experiences (your thoughts and behaviors, messages from others) that might be maintaining your dissatisfaction. Now add a list of how your body image affects your life. Look at Katy's list (below).

Katy's body image

How did my negative body image develop?
When I was young, Mum was overweight and often on a diet. She used to tell me not to eat too many sweets. I reached puberty early and remember the boys at school teasing me about my shape. I remember my first "serious" boyfriend used to always criticize my appearance. That was when I really started to hate my body. I used to watch films and think all the actresses looked so thin and pretty.

What maintains my body dissatisfaction?
My friends tell me that I am always putting myself down and ignoring my good features. I know that I always compare myself to others and cannot listen to compliments about myself. I wear baggy clothes to hide myself. I do a lot of body-checking and weigh myself frequently to try and stay in control.

How does this affect my life?
It makes me very unhappy – I never feel good enough. I get anxious seeing friends or going to parties as I wonder what others will think of me – sometimes I cancel altogether. I avoid relationships as I couldn't bear for anyone to see my body.

Looking at your notes, you are likely to see the familiar hot cross bun pattern that we have described above – your thoughts, feelings, perceptions of yourself, and behaviors are all linked. Negative thoughts, feelings, and behaviors will all perpetuate your negative body image. For example, Katy realized that she only focused on the worst parts of her appearance, while ignoring compliments from others and failing to attend to the parts that she thought were OK.

Beginning to change your relationship with your body

As we said above, the goal is to work towards acceptance of your body rather than complete satisfaction. This means moving away from a position whereby self-criticism and anxiety regarding your appearance dominate your life. Of course, there may still be occasions when you do not feel entirely happy with your appearance – that is a normal experience. However, such thoughts will not rule your life in the way that they do now.

Take some time to think about how you relate to your body now. Do you tend to see it as an inconvenience? Something that never does what you want it to do? Something that lets you down? We suggest you try the following letter-writing task.

First, take ten minutes to write a letter from your body to you. Allow your body to express how it feels about the way you treat it. When you have written the letter, take time to reflect on how you feel. Then, write a kind and compassionate letter back to your body, explaining how you intend to treat it in the future. In particular, think about what your body does for you and the parts that you do like. Jenny wrote the following letter:

Dear Jenny
I always feel that I have let you down, that I am not good enough for you. For the last 14 years, I have always been starved and not able to operate at my best, yet you have kept me in the gym, pounding away until my joints ached. I am beginning to decay. I can't have children and my bones are weakening, yet this is still not enough. All these years, I have carried you through, kept you alive, and enabled you to do all these amazing things. You neglect me and often insist on keeping me cold just to burn off more kilocalories.
    Your body

Jenny then wrote the following letter back:

Dear body
Thank you for your letter. I had not thought before about all that you do for me – you keep me alive, you keep me breathing, you enable me to share hugs and affection. You get me to the places I need to be so that I can do the things I want to do. I realize that I have been too focused on the numbers on the scale rather than appreciating all the other things that you do for me. I have been critical and punishing towards you when you haven't done anything wrong. I realize that I have inflicted a lot of damage on you, although as I have begun to eat more healthily and regularly, hopefully some of this will be reversed. I have already noticed that my skin is becoming less dry and my hair is in better condition. In the future, I will try and treat you more kindly, to eat normally, and to cut back on my excessive exercise.
    Jenny

Table 9.6

Behavior	*Do I do this a lot?* (1=not at all; 5=all the time)
I wear baggy clothes and avoid wearing anything fitted (e.g., swimsuit, fitted dress).	
I have removed all mirrors from my home and I avoid reflective surfaces.	
It takes me a long time to decide what to wear.	
I have kept all my clothes from when I was underweight – just in case I can fit into them in the future.	
I avoid looking at myself in the shower or bath and/or avoid self-care such as moisturizing myself	
I compare my weight to that of friends, celebrities or other people I see.	
It would be unacceptable for me to leave the house without full make-up or grooming.	
When I go out, for example to a café or on public transport, I will always notice the thinnest person there, and overlook everybody else.	
I repeatedly check my appearance (e.g., in mirrors, reflective surfaces).	
It is very hard for me to spend money on new clothes for myself – many of my clothes are worn or have holes.	

Practical steps to addressing your body image

Many people find they have developed a number of behaviors to avoid their bodies or to compensate for how they feel about their bodies. Look at the list (Table 9.6) above to see if any of these are familiar:

Looking at this list, you will see that the behaviors broadly fall into four groups – avoidance of your body, checking your body/appearance, camouflaging your body/compensating for what you believe you look like (e.g., spending a lot of time or money to look good, but frequently still feeling dissatisfied or insecure), and comparing with others. Most people don't use all these behaviors, and do not use them all the time. More often, you will probably use a constellation of behaviors according to the situation. These behaviors all maintain your negative body image by drawing your attention towards what you dislike and away from what you think is OK.

Use this list to begin to think about what you need to change in order to accept your body. You can do this in ways that were described earlier in this section – exposure, behavioral experiments and surveys (see below).

Exposure

For example, Katy was very anxious about what others thought about her, and therefore tended to cover up in baggy, dark clothing. To address this anxiety, she decided to develop an exposure hierarchy (a way of getting closer and closer to the thing that she feared, but doing it in small steps so that her anxiety had a chance to subside, allowing her to learn that the feared object is not so scary after all). She made a list of changes she wanted to make, ordered in increasing levels of difficulty. That list began with wearing a slightly more fitted top, and rose to wearing a dress on a night out. She worked gradually through the list, moving to the next stage as her anxiety decreased.

In a similar vein, Jenny tried to avoid looking at or thinking about her body at all costs. She developed an exposure hierarchy that started with looking in the mirror at least once a day. This list progressed to increased self-care (e.g., using body lotion and make-up). Her final challenge was to visit the hairdresser's for a professional hair cut, something she had not allowed herself to do for many years.

Behavioral experiments

When thinking about changing body image, as with other aspects of your eating problems (see Step 3 of this program), behavioral experiments can be a very powerful method of challenging your beliefs. In some cases, you can directly test your beliefs and compare them with less distressing alternatives. As with any such belief, it is important to consider whether you are right or not, and to set up the conditions in a way that will allow you to test your belief. You can use the behavioral experiments sheet from Appendix 19 to do this, as before.

As an example, Polly's concerns about her weight and shape revolved around very strong beliefs such as: "If I eat bread, then my stomach will swell up hugely." Further questioning showed that she meant her waist (many individuals belief that their stomach is much lower down their body than it is actually located). After planning with her, this belief was tested by asking Polly to measure her waist (using a tape measure) before and after eating a small amount of bread, and discovering whether her waist size had increased by the amount that she predicted. In general, her finding was that her waist size remained unchanged. Continuing her experimentation, she tested this belief further by examining: whether larger amounts of bread (up to two slices) had this effect; whether different types of bread had different effects; and whether the time after eating the bread made a difference. As the findings were negative, she ended up much less convinced by her original belief, and able to see that the alternative belief ("My stomach feels bigger because I am more anxious, and I am picking up my anxiety and assuming that I have got bigger") was more probable.

Behavioral experiments are also useful for testing out the value of body-related behaviors, such as avoidance, checking and comparison. For example, Katy's repeated use of her weighing scales to calm herself had the potential long-term impact of making her more anxious and hence feeling worse about her appearance (weighing herself had become a safety behavior). Her fear was that she would become much more anxious and gain weight if she did not weigh herself repeatedly. This meant that she could not go out for any length of time or eat outside the house, for fear of not being able to calm herself by checking her weight. The behavioral experiment in this case was to try out her normal pattern of weighing herself for a week, then to try out *not* body-checking in this way for a week, to see whether her anxiety at not weighing herself was sustained and whether her weight went up (as she predicted). The result was that she found her overall level of anxiety was much lower across the week when she did not weigh herself, and that her weight did not shift at all over that time (rather than going up by the 5 kg that she had predicted). This led her to the conclusion that her body-checking was actually harming her, rather than being the support that she believed.

Surveys

A particular issue can be when you "mind read" what others think about your appearance. In other words, you assume that others think negatively about your appearance, but that they would not say anything about it. Of course, trying to challenge your beliefs using methods such as behavioral experiments is unlikely to be effective in such circumstances, because you believe that you cannot get genuine feedback if others are unwilling to tell you what they really believe or feel about your appearance.

One technique that can be helpful in such circumstances is the *survey.* When conducting a survey, you ask others to make judgements about you (e.g., rating a photo of you), and see if what they say matches your beliefs about their views of your appearance. If this is a scary thought, then you can ask a relative or a friend to do the work of showing your photos. As an example, you could do the following:

1. Pick some photos that you think show you realistically as you are now.
2. Write down what you think others will say when they see the photos, and rate how certain you are that they will say that (e.g., "I am 80% certain that they will think that I look pregnant, and I believe that they will say that I am at least an 8 on a 1–10 scale of fatness").
3. Get others (at least ten people) to rate the photos anonymously. This is often much easier to do if you ask a friend or relative to do it for you, as long as you agree that they have to pass on the full set of answers and not censor them.
4. Compare what you thought those people would say with what they actually said. The most common outcome is that you realize that other's views of your appearance and what it says about you (e.g., size, attractiveness, personality) are completely different from what you believe they must be thinking. In other words, you get to find out if your "mind-reading" is right or wrong

(e.g., "They rated me as a 4 on that 1–10 scale, and most of the comments were about how slim I look or what I was wearing. Nobody said that I looked pregnant, even though I thought that about eight of the ten would have said that about me in that photo").

5. Go back to the beginning, review your beliefs, and consider another survey to push your beliefs even harder (e.g., "Maybe those first results were only positive because I hide myself well with make-up, clothes, etc. If I tried another survey, with a photo where I was not wearing make-up, then they would see the real me – just as awful as I think I must look to them"). The more often you do this, the less anxious you will become as you start processing your own appearance as other people do.

This survey technique can be extended according to your concerns. For example, if you have gained weight and you feel that this has made you look worse, then you can compare how people react to photos from before your weight gain with how they judge your current appearance in photos. When Jenny did this, it resulted in the following conclusion:

> I was sure that they would say that I looked better in the old photos, but they all said that I look much better in the new ones. What's more, they said that I looked too skinny back then and that I still look slim now, even though I thought they would say I was chubby back then and just plain fat now.

You can use this method to address a range of such concerns about how others see you (e.g., do women judge you differently to men; how do people see you in comparison with your friends?).

A final note about body image

We have emphasized that it can take time to see an improvement in the way you feel about your body. You will probably need to keep revisiting this section of the book over time, in order to continue working on your worries about your appearance. Remember most people (if not all) are dissatisfied with some aspect of their physical appearance, but those who are able to accept their bodies are the ones who are able to see its less desirable physical parts as a part of their whole self, which consists of many different aspects that are positive, negative, and neutral.

Step 5: Addressing residual difficulties

"I am eating more healthily now, but there are still some things that I am worried about."

Simply getting your eating healthy again will not necessarily lead to all the changes that you need. While treating the eating disorder can have the effect of improving/stabilizing your mood and making you less depressed and anxious, it is possible that you will have other problems (e.g., anxieties about being in social situations) that remain after this course of CBT. If you have used this program in the way it was intended, then it is likely that you can use other self-help approaches for those problems. A range of self-help CBT books exists to help with such problems, and a useful selection is given in the "Further Reading" list. See Section 6 for more information on this.

The three most common general residual issues that sufferers report at the end of any course of CBT are emotional instability, perfectionism, and low self-esteem. All three should improve as a result of the self-help approach described here. However, it may be that you need to seek additional help or support, in which case you may want to have a look at Section 5 of this book, which describes how to access formal treatment.

Step 6: Maintaining the gains

"I am sort of forgetting what it was like to wake up every morning with the eating disorder hanging over my head."

By now, if you have been making the changes, you are likely to be feeling much more relaxed, happy, and comfortable with your eating, weight, and shape. However, you cannot assume that there is no work left to do. Maintaining the gains is a key stage in eating healthily again. We deal with this in more detail in Section 6 of this book, but here are a couple of key points for you to consider.

Keep yourself aware of what you are doing and the risks

There are many ways in which you can consolidate your improvements and continue to develop. You should maintain the personal therapy sessions, though you might start spacing them out to fortnightly then monthly for several months. At each therapy session, you should consider the following points:
• What am I doing well?
• What can I safely stop doing? (e.g., it is often a good idea to keep using the food diary for a quite a while even after your eating behaviors have stopped and you feel that you have recovered from your eating disorder. On the other hand, stopping the diary-keeping can help you to find out whether your eating problems will or will not return. They will be less likely to if you have done all the above, but you will ultimately need to find this out for yourself).
• Have any of my symptoms come back since last time? If so, what worked before, have I stopped doing it, and do I need to go back to that? (e.g., did you binge over the past two weeks, and does it indicate that you need to go back to a more structured diet?).

- Am I losing weight? Is it taking me down below a healthy level (i.e., a sign of sliding back into restriction/anorexia)?
- How am I doing on the short- and long-term goals for therapy that I set at the beginning of this process? Do I need to revise those goals because I have changed my mind, or do I need to modify my progress to get to them?

When can I stop therapy?

As we said earlier, that is hard to define. Maybe it will be when you have stretched your therapy sessions so far apart that you get a shock when one comes along. Maybe it will be when you cannot remember the last time that you worried about your eating, weight, and shape. Revisit your therapy goals from Section 2, and decide whether you have met all the ones that you wanted to (remember that your goals might have changed over time, and some might now seem less important, and some new ones might have been achieved without your realizing that they were issues for you). If you are not sure, then tell your relatives or friends that you are thinking about stopping therapy, and ask them if that makes sense to them. You might just find that they have almost forgotten that you ever had the problem. That is a really good sign that you have changed, and that it is time to put this book and your treatment book aside (somewhere you can find them – see below). We could all benefit from putting some time aside for ourselves to think about our achievements and to take time to resolve the things that are bothering us, so maybe reduce frequency and shift the content of the sessions but continue having them for as long as feels helpful (even if eating is not a focus anymore).

What if I lapse in the future?

Again, this is dealt with in far more depth in Section 6. For now, just think of this one practical point: when putting this book and your therapy notebook aside, make sure that you know where they are. If you ever worry that you might be slipping back into using your eating behaviors, get out your notebook and review all that you have done here. Consider carefully whether you already have the solutions to any problems that have returned, and use the skills that you learned here. Be honest with yourself, and act fast. That is the surest way to get back in control, and to stop a lapse becoming a relapse.

Where to next in this book?

If you are a sufferer, you might find the material outlined in Section 6 – letting go of your eating problem – to be most directly relevant and useful to you. However, it will also be helpful for you to know the material in the forthcoming Section 4, and we would advise that you read that section in order to get an understanding of the experiences of those around you who might also have been affected by your eating problem. In many ways, we hope that you do not need Section 5, which is about how to get the best kind of formal help if the self-help approach is not enough. However, if the self-help program here is not enough, then Section 5 will give you important information about your options and what to look for when considering professional help.

For carers

If you are reading this section, then you are involved in caring for an individual suffering from an eating disorder (or you are the sufferer, wanting to understand the impact of your problem on those around you). We use the term "carers" broadly to describe anyone who plays a significant role in the sufferer's life, including parents, partners, siblings, children, extended family, and friends.

Caring for an individual with an eating disorder has a major impact on loved ones. Carers have substantial difficulties in their role (e.g., Highet *et al.*, 2005; Treasure *et al.*, 2001), including:

- managing emotional distress (their own and the sufferer's)
- managing negative behaviors
- financial costs
- stigma
- problems with services
- managing the extent of changes to their lives

Some carers report positive outcomes, such as having developed enhanced personal qualities (e.g., empathy towards the problems of others) and a sense of value from helping the sufferer. However, the balance of positive and negative outcomes tends to be very negative for the carer.

Recovery from an eating disorder takes a significant effort from the sufferer and their carers, especially as the course of the illness is often long and drawn out. Therefore, it is vital that any effort to help the individual with the eating disorder provides as much support to those around them. This section outlines understanding, skills, and tools that we have found helpful for carers as they share the journey with their loved one.

10

Am I to blame for the eating problem?

One of the difficulties in caring for someone with an eating disorder is that you might believe you are in some way responsible for the eating disorder. This is commonly the case for the parents of the individual with the eating disorder, but it can also affect other carers, such as partners, siblings, and even children of the sufferer. You can get caught up in asking yourself questions to which there are no answers (e.g., "What if I had not made that comment about how she looked?"; "Maybe I should not have gone on that diet, and then things would have turned out differently"; "What did I do wrong?"). In the past, such self-blame has been propped up by theorists who have described the eating disorders as having their origins in family styles. Therefore, it is vital that we are clear about this issue.

Stop blaming yourself

The research literature shows that there is no one single factor that causes an eating disorder. Even in multi-factorial models of eating problems, the evidence that families play any role at all in the development of those problems is weak at best. Certainly, it is true that the families of eating disorder sufferers commonly have problems in their interactional style, but those problems can be seen as the *result* of there being a family member with an eating disorder, rather than the *cause*.

Blaming yourself for the eating disorder can inadvertently result in the strengthening of the eating disorder. You might feel guilt as a result of blaming yourself for the eating disorder, but that guilt can be unhelpful, and can lead you to try to protect the sufferer from facing the consequences of the problem behavior (e.g., replacing food taken in a binge; not raising concerns about weight loss). If you are experiencing guilt, ask yourself: "Am I am taking responsibility for something that I can do nothing about, and if so then would my energy be better spent helping my daughter/friend/partner get better rather than beating myself up?"

If you can identify things that you do that might be maintaining the sufferer's eating disorder, then write them down and share them with other carers and with the sufferer. Discuss what would happen if you stopped those behaviors, and when you might do this.

For example, Katy's mother felt guilty because she had often gone on diets with her daughter. She was aware that Katy had begun to binge and then vomit during their last joint diet. As she felt guilty about encouraging Katy to diet, she had been replacing all the food that had been going missing from the pantry. When she began to read information about bulimia she realized there were multiple reasons that Katy might have developed her eating disorder. She thought about what behaviors Katy was engaging in and how her own guilt had stopped her from making Katy face up to her behavior. Katy's mother saw her own behaviors (e.g., replacing food that Katy had binged on; cleaning the bathroom after Katy had been sick) as having been a problem. She had never talked to anyone in the family about this, including her husband. She decided to talk with Katy, simply stating that she wanted to support her in seeking help, although she knew that this might not be what Katy wanted at this stage. However, she also stated that she would no longer be replacing the food eaten in a binge or cleaning up after Katy, leaving these as Katy's responsibility.

Why didn't I notice before?

You are very likely to ask yourself whether you should have noticed the eating disorder earlier. However, there are several reasons that this can be difficult:
• not knowing what to look for
• the sufferer denying any problem, so that their control is not threatened
• the sufferer hiding the extent of the problem, out of shame and embarrassment, and a desire to spare their loved ones from the stress

These are the same experiences that many clinicians have when first meeting a sufferer, and even the most experienced clinician can be led into thinking there is no real problem. Given how hard it is to identify an eating disorder, you should give yourself a break about this issue, and move forward to supporting the sufferer.

11

What can I do to support the sufferer?

There are many things that you can do to support the sufferer, but to be able to do that you will need to support yourself too. You will be of little help to anyone if you are too distressed to think straight. Think about some of the arguments that you might have had with the sufferer, and the sleepless nights. Those will tell you that the emotions can become overwhelming. First, you will all need to deal with the emotional consequences of the eating disorder.

Dealing with emotional distress

Clearly, as a carer you are likely to experience a range of emotions – including anxiety and worry about the sufferer, sadness for everybody's impaired lives, and anger and frustration at the sufferer's apparent stuck position. First, you need to be clear which of these emotions you are feeling and what you can realistically do about them. Your personal style of handling emotions might be positive or negative, depending on the sufferer and the situation. If emotional clashes are a feature of your relationship with the sufferer, then we recommend that you read the book by Treasure *et al.* (2007 – see the reference list), which covers this topic in depth.

It is important to remember that emotions reduce when they have reached their peak. If you allow yourself or the sufferer to experience your sadness or anger rather than trying to battle or hide it, your distress will be reduced. If you avoid the emotional state by hiding it from yourself or others, then it will come back and hit you harder.

Should I feel so stressed and impotent?

Eating disorders serve a function in the sufferer's life (e.g., feeling in control; emotional suppression). This means that the sufferer may be unwilling to give up their behaviors, and may be in denial about the seriousness of their symptoms. Therefore, they are often resentful and angry about offers of help. Under these circumstances, it is natural that you will feel stressed and powerless. The question is, what support can you get to help you reduce the sense of powerlessness? Ways of doing this can include:

- getting better educated about the problem (e.g., reading the psychoeducation appendices at the back of this book)
- accessing support of some sort (e.g., carer groups, internet support)
- making time for yourself and your other relationships (e.g., letting yourself have a supportive relationship; taking time out to do things that you enjoy). In short, you need to have a life to get back to. Sometimes, all that effort that you put into caring for the sufferer means that you stop taking care of yourself, and that makes you of no use to yourself or anybody else (e.g., if you are putting 110 % into your youngest daughter's needs, that means you do not have time to be a parent to your other children, or to take care of your partner or yourself).

How do I talk to the sufferer?

Talking to an individual about their eating disorder can be a frightening and stressful process. The sufferer might be angry at being asked about their eating disorder, making them hostile to any initial approach. However, our experience is that this is only an initial reaction, and that if you persist in a supportive way then most sufferers come to appreciate the fact that someone cares enough to approach them about the problem and to persevere. Before approaching the sufferer, it is worth asking the following questions:

- Am I the best person to approach the sufferer? It may be someone else in or outside the family is currently best placed to talk with the sufferer or to assist you in the process.
- When is the best time to approach the sufferer? It is worth considering when would be the worst time to talk to the sufferer, and avoiding such times (e.g., over meals; when you are likely to be interrupted).
- What should I say? Finally, taking the time to think about what you are going to say is essential. It can help to practice what you are going to say with a family member or friend, and ask them to role-play a variety of responses, so that you can remain calm and focused on your task when actually talking to the sufferer.

Dangers of collusion

When caring for someone with an eating disorder there are several patterns of behaviors that you can get into that collude with and strengthen the eating disorder. The first is to act as if the eating disorder is a *secret* – ignoring the behavior (and the associated emotion and thinking) or discounting its very serious nature, and thus allowing it to continue. Ignoring behaviors seems to be a very normal human reaction to difficult problems. We often ignore behavior in the hope that the problem will resolve itself, especially given that efforts in the past to discuss the problem might have resulted in denial or hostility. Unfortunately, we know that eating disorders rarely resolve themselves, and the longer the sufferer has the problem the harder it can be to get better.

A sense of frustration and anger at the individual's lack of desire to change in the face of extreme risk of physical harm can lead to the carer attempting to *take control* of the sufferer's behavior, for example, trying to force the individual to eat. While this behavior is understandable, given the very natural concern about the sufferer, attempts by others to take control can force the sufferer further into the disorder (e.g., driving them into lying about their behavior or finding a way to compensate later on). One of the functions of an eating disorder can be to provide the sufferer with a sense of control over the world. In attempting to take over as a carer, the sufferer is likely to feel that their control is being taken away, leading to further attempts to regain that control (e.g., through use of further eating disorder behavior).

Finally, carers commonly try to *compensate* for the disorder. This pattern is seen when carers adapt to the eating-disordered behavior (e.g., agreeing when their daughter insists that the whole family should do without butter in the refrigerator in order to reduce her fear of contamination; allowing their daughter to set portion sizes for everybody in the family and to serve everybody's food to ensure this). Such compensation can be driven by a sense of guilt or by a mistaken belief that it helps the sufferer. However, while it can help the sufferer in the short term (e.g., reducing their anxiety about weight gain), it maintains the behavior in the long term by keeping the patient fearful of change.

In short, it is worth asking the questions: "Am I am colluding with the eating disorder?" and, if the answer is yes, "How can I work to stop this behavior?" Often, getting the opinion of a trusted friend who is outside the situation can help to get some perspective on this issue.

What about the rest of the family?

Many people in a family can be affected by someone suffering from an eating disorder – probably more so when there is more direct contact with the sufferer. Our experience is that eating disorders tend to take whole families hostage, rather than controlling only the sufferer. In short, other members of the family can be neglected while you all spend energy battling the eating disorder. Talk to other family members about what is going on, and be as open and honest as possible. Your aim is to build a strong family unit against the eating disorder. This strategy is helpful because it lets the family unite against the eating disorder rather than against the sufferer. This can involve even apparently trivial involvement (e.g., helping to distract the sufferer by playing a board game after a meal).

What can I do if I am worried about the sufferer?

If you are worried about the sufferer, then talk to her or him about your concerns. As you have learned earlier in this book, all individuals with an eating disorder are at some degree of physical risk. Even if they do not want to be actively working on changing their eating disorder at the present time, they should be having regular physical monitoring with their family doctor. They might be more willing to go to the doctor for such physical monitoring if there was no pressure to attend further services or make other changes. However, if they are not prepared to see their doctor, then go to the doctor yourself in order to share your fears or get advice. If you are not sure what to say to your doctor, then try contacting your local self-help organizations for a chance to talk about what you might say in order to feel less out of control. In extreme circumstances, your doctor might want you to be ready to engage with emergency medical and psychiatric services, for the sufferer's safety. Just finding out whether or not your doctor is that concerned can be a great relief for you.

If the sufferer is already in treatment for their eating disorder, then you might be able to speak to their therapist. However, it is unlikely that they will be able to give you much information, as the sufferer has rights to confidentiality. However, the therapist can listen to what you have to say. Try to get a feel for whether the therapist feels like a "safe" person, who would be likely to take action if there were any concerns about the sufferer being at risk of self-harm or at physical risk. Many services will be keen to work with carers to help support the individual with the eating disorder and, if you and your loved one wish, will offer a joint appointment with you and the sufferer.

How to ask for help and who to ask?

Sometimes it is difficult to ask for help. Carers believe they may be making a "fuss about nothing." However, it has never been our experience that carers are getting worked up about trivial issues. Carers often delay taking action because they feel conflict about seeking help, as the onset of an eating disorder is slow – when exactly is the day that one should be worrying about weight loss? This problem can be made worse by the fact that sufferers can often conceal the true extent of their problems (e.g., "I ate earlier"). If you have even a mild suspicion and you are worried that the sufferer is not being open with you, then call an eating disorders helpline and discuss your concerns. They should be able to give you advice on how to approach your family doctor (e.g., what information to give) and might put you in contact with other carers so that you can share experiences and ask questions.

Where can I get information?

First, read the psychoeducation material in this book (see Appendices 2–16). It will tell you a lot of what you need to know about eating disorders, which should help you to understand more about the key features of the sufferer's problems.

There are many excellent organizations dedicated to providing information and support to carers and sufferers of eating disorders. All can be easily located on the internet, but see Appendix 1 for a list of these.

Getting help for yourself

An essential part of providing the best care for someone with an eating disorder is making sure that you are robust enough to do so. Caring for someone with an eating disorder is extremely stressful, and it is no surprise that you might need help. This might mean that you need to seek out support for you and your family. Such help might take the form of attending a support group for carers, individual sessions with a trained professional, respite care, or more formal family therapy with yourselves and the sufferer.

A carers' support group will enable you to talk about the difficulties involved in caring for someone with a mental health problem, with people who may have experienced the same issues. Families often report that talking with someone who has "walked in their shoes" is extremely helpful for support, encouragement, and practical strategies.

How can I keep the sufferer interested in change?

Once you have taken the first step of ensuring that the sufferer's physical health is being monitored by a relevant professional, then you can focus on the task of working with the sufferer to help them think about change. But that can be a complex business. The most important issue in keeping the sufferer interested in change is to understand how and why people change. Change is a process, rather than a one-off event. It is normal for individuals' levels of motivation to fluctuate, and your loved one might consider making a change one day but by the next day that motivation appears to have vanished. Your task is to respond in a way that lets the sufferer move forward overall, even if a particular day contains a setback.

One critical issue is when the sufferer gets mixed messages from their different carers (e.g., where one parent is gentle and supportive, but another is firmer and pushes for change). The combination of different carer responses can cause greater difficulties and confusion, resulting in carers clashing too. So make sure that you sit down with other carers and agree what your response will be as a consistent "team." This will mean that some carers have to tone their responses down while others have to be firmer, but this will be necessary to achieve the bigger goal – help for the sufferer.

Considering the motivational states outlined in Chapter 5, how can you help the person to move to the more productive states, where positive change can happen? The key skills are helping the sufferer to deal with those states where they are not actively trying to change.

If the sufferer is in an *"anti-contemplative" state* and remains relatively stable or healthy (see the beginning of Chapter 5), then it might be necessary for them to experience failure in some important ways (e.g., poor school results; problems in relationships) before they will consider whether there is something wrong. However, we find that it can be helpful to push the sufferer by saying that you think there is a problem, then saying that you are pulling back (without agreeing that there is no problem). This means that you have raised your concerns for the sufferer to be aware of them, but you have avoided the fight that the sufferer would normally get you into (in order to get you to back down). Maybe a letter to the sufferer would help, where you say what you are worried about (e.g., "You look painfully thin"; "Others are asking us if you are all right"; "We hear you vomiting after meals"), making it clear that you are not looking for a fight, and offering to chat when the sufferer is ready (or to find outside help, if that is preferred).

If the sufferer is in a *"pre-contemplative"* state, attempting to force them to change can result in their digging in and defending their position. Before you act, take a moment to think about a time when someone asked you to change something and you were not ready to change. How did that feel? Did having pressure put upon you mean you were more or less likely to change? Did you find yourself listing all the reasons in your head for not changing? If they are not ready, people feel a sense of resistance when being asked to change. Treasure and Schmidt (2008) use one of Aesop's fables to convey this idea to carers.

> The sun and the wind were having a dispute as to who was the most powerful. They saw a man walking along and they challenged each other about which of them would be most successful at getting the man to remove his coat. The wind started first and blew up a huge gale; the coat flapped but the man only closed all his buttons and tightened up his belt. The sun tried next and shone brightly, making the man sweat. He proceeded to take off his coat.

What promotes change is the sufferer developing their own reasons for change rather than accepting someone else's. It is also important to remember that ultimately the responsibility for change lies with the individual. The best way to assist someone in the pre-contemplation state of change is to acknowledge that they are not ready to change and that the decision is theirs, but make it clear that you are happy to listen to the sufferer about their problem, even though they are not ready to talk about it yet. The aim is to encourage self-exploration rather than action. Supporting the person by listening to them enables them to start to explore some of their reasons for thinking about change. On the surface, listening seems like an easy skill. However, to listen takes several skills. We would encourage you to become an "active listener" – one who conveys respect to the person and shows understanding. There are four key elements of active listening. These are:
1. Give your undivided attention and show that you are listening by using your own body language (e.g., nodding in response to points made).
2. Provide feedback by reflecting back what is said and ask questions (e.g., "It sounds like you are saying..." or "Tell me more about..."). It is also useful to summarize the speaker's comments.

3. Don't interrupt – wait until the speaker indicates that she or he is ready to hear your response.
4. Respond appropriately by being respectful of the person's position. In the case of recovery from an eating disorder, there is no easy solution. This message can be conveyed by simply reflecting on the hard position that the sufferer is in, rather than asking the sufferer to come up with a solution. For example, "It sounds like things are really tough for you right now" or "I can see that you are trying really hard here."

Over time, consistent support and listening can help the person generate their own arguments for making a change.

Where the sufferer is in a "contemplative" state, he or she is ready to take in more information about the possible change, and is more interested in the topic in general (e.g., thinking that they might make changes soon, though not just yet). They are more aware of the "pros" of changing, but are also acutely aware of the "cons." Although such contemplation can be encouraging to the carer, sufferers can remain stuck in this state for long periods of time, trapped by the ambivalence created by the balance between costs and benefits of change or by the fear of failing to change successfully (e.g., "What if I change my eating and life just gets worse?"). It is time to use those non-judgemental listening skills (see above) to let the individual contemplate those "pros" and "cons." It can be helpful to break those "pros" and "cons" into the short and long term. We have outlined what this might look like in an earlier chapter (Chapter 5). It can be valuable to ask your loved one to go over this exercise with you, and particularly to contemplate the imbalance between short- and long-term outcomes (usually, the "pros" are mostly short-term, while the "cons" tend to be longer-term). Get the sufferer to look upon their eating behaviors as being a trade-off – short-term safety (with the consequence of long-term "stuckness" and depression) versus long-term development (with the consequence of short-term anxiety while change happens and the endpoint seeming hard to be sure about).

Of course, you can still help when the sufferer is in a state of *preparation, change,* or *maintenance* (see Chapter 5), but such assistance is largely about helping the sufferer take the steps they need towards personal change. You will find that the skills of non-judgemental listening (outlined above) are helpful here, but that you need to offer more active support at times (e.g., changing what food you buy for the sufferer, so that it is more like the rest of the family's diet).

I am a friend of the sufferer: how can I help?

If you are a friend of someone with an eating disorder, you will obviously want to help. As with other carers, the lead as to what you can do to help should come from the sufferer, and techniques for listening helpfully are outlined in the previous subsection. The sufferer will be able to let you know what they find helpful. Aside from these guidelines, the most help you can give is the obvious – be a good friend. Continue to do fun activities together, accepting the person for whom they are and listening when times get tough. However, you also need to be honest with the sufferer at times (e.g., "I don't think it is a good idea for us to go on holiday together, as I don't feel skilled enough to cope if you have a medical crisis"). The value of your role as a friend cannot be overestimated, as it enables the sufferer to see more of themselves as they might be without the eating disorder.

Sufferers with chronic disorders

Sadly, some individuals have had their eating disorder for a long time, but we still find that change is possible, no matter how long they have had their eating problem. For some, the focus of change may be different (e.g., instead of changing eating behaviors, the focus might be on making other changes in order to improve quality of life). For example, Nonie had suffered from anorexia nervosa for seventeen years. She did not want to change any aspect of her eating, but she wanted something to look forward to on the days when she was not doing her part-time job. With the support of her mother, she searched for a community activity. In the end, one day a week she joined the local library book group. She found she felt more able to get out of bed on that day, and she enjoyed the contact with other members of the group. Her older brother also helped out by meeting her on a more regular basis for coffee, and she joined a pottery class with her niece. She also met her family doctor for a check up once a year, as suggested in the National Institute for Health and Clinical Excellence (NICE, 2004) guidelines.

Supporting the sufferer while they are following the self-help program outlined in this book

First, it is important for you as a carer to understand the demands of the CBT approach. Cognitive behavioral therapy is a demanding treatment, requiring the individual to work hard, and the sufferer will need all the help and support that you can give them. The details of the approach are given earlier in this book, so please read it. If the sufferer is not following the program in the way it is intended, you might need to remind them that this evidence-based approach depends on doing the work.

The best way to support the sufferer while they are going through the self-help period is to ask them what would be helpful. The sufferer might want to discuss each weekly session held, and might want assistance with planning and monitoring homework. Alternatively, they might be asking for direct practical help, such as help in determining normal portion sizes.

Remember, this will not be a smooth process. As new challenges occur throughout treatment, the sufferer might decide it is too hard to change at this point in time and slip back into previous behaviors. This is very normal and your

Table 11.1 Questionnaire 2b: Does my relative/child/partner/parent/friend have an eating problem, and how is it affecting her/his life and mine?

Just tick the answer that most closely describes your feelings on each of these points. Because this questionnaire is for all types of sufferer, we have not specified who the sufferer is (e.g., your child, your partner, your friend, or your parent)	Not at all	A little	Sometimes	Most of the time	All of the time
The sufferer's eating controls her/his life					
The sufferer feels that she/he is in control of her/his eating, but that is not the case					
My relationship with the sufferer is poorer because of her/his eating pattern					
My relationship with the sufferer is stressful because of issues around food and eating					
My life is constrained by the sufferer's eating and body concerns and related behaviors					
I wish that I could have a normal relationship with the sufferer, untainted by food					
Our whole relationship is influenced by the sufferer's eating					
I can see that the sufferer's quality of life is really suffering, and she or he is not developing as she/he could					
The sufferer's eating takes up so much of her/his time, that she/he has no time for a happy life					
I am stressed by the sufferer's eating problems and how they affect her/his behavior					
My own eating suffers as a result of the sufferer's rules and behaviors about food					
My other relationships are damaged by the sufferer's eating problems					

role in this case should be to support the person until they are ready to think about moving forward again.

So has all your work helped? Let us go back to those questions from Chapter 1, and compare your feelings after the treatment program (see Table 11.1 above) with how things seemed back then. If the sufferer is happy to compare notes, then look at whether they have changed more or less than you have.

Transitions into more formal help

So what if you are a sufferer, you have tried everything in the earlier part of this book and you still feel that it's not working? Or that doing it on your own is just too difficult? What if you are a carer who has watched your loved one struggling to achieve change, but you fear that their best efforts are not enough?

You are not alone. Many sufferers reading self-help guides find that they cannot implement them on their own, or that they manage to implement these strategies for a certain amount of time (often quite successfully), but then fall back into their old eating habits. While self-help books do contain strategies that can really help you to get better, putting them into action by yourself can be difficult. So in this section, we want to give you some tips on how you can start seeking out some professional help, if you feel that doing it alone or with the support of your partner, friends, and/or relatives is not working.

Before you go any further

Just one thing for the sufferer to consider first. Before you read this section, go back and look at what you have done so far, preferably with your carer. Review what you have done, and ask yourself whether you can spot ways in which you might have let some core changes slide. Some examples are:

- "Well, I tried very hard, but never actually changed my eating. I treated that bit as optional".
- "I wanted everything to be different within a week, so I sort of gave up after that".
- "I told my family that I was changing when I was not really doing so".
- "I treated bingeing as being OK – I kept doing it, but kind of fooled myself that it didn't count".
- "I turned to this section first, rather than doing the stuff in earlier sections of the book".

If any of these sound familiar, then it might be worth revisiting the CBT program, and thinking about trying to do all of it, rather than only the parts you feel more comfortable with (usually the bits that do not involve changing your eating).

That does not mean that you cannot seek more formal help, but remember that you can do two things at once – self-help and starting the process of being referred for formal help. Indeed, revisiting the self-help approach is very helpful to give you a good head start when you enter treatment.

A key thing to remember is that not having succeeded in self-help CBT is not at all an indicator that you are a failure. Many people who fail to benefit from a self-help approach to treatment go on to do well in individual treatment with a clinician. Nor does it mean that CBT cannot work for you – on average, self-help is not as effective as therapy with a clinician, and many people do well with individual CBT after not benefiting from their self-help efforts. You have lost nothing by trying the self-help route, as long as you have maintained your physical health through collaboration with your doctor.

12

Thinking about getting more formal therapeutic help

First, let's consider when you might start looking for professional help. The obvious answer might seem to be: "When the self help approach is clearly not working." However, we are not always rational beings. One of the biggest challenges to moving from self-help into formal treatment is tackling the prejudices that you or others may hold about such treatment. It is very normal to be anxious about accessing more formal treatment, and sufferers of eating disorders will commonly have had the disorder for many years before they consider approaching their doctor about a referral to mental health services.

What has stopped me seeking help before, and what might stop me now?

This failure to seek treatment is often because of the beliefs that people have about treatment. Some common beliefs or prejudices that sufferers and carers hold are:

"People will think I am crazy." This is a major concern for those seeking formal help for their eating disorder. Those people can include family, friends, and workmates, as well as health professionals who may assess your problem (see below). It is true there is significant stigma in society attached to having a mental health problem. However, our experience is that when sufferers have chosen to share with others that they are seeking treatment, they have received support and encouragement in return. Many people know someone with an eating disorder, and know that these problems merit help and understanding.

"Seeking formal help will show me to be silly or unable to take care of myself." Attending formal treatment will enable you to understand your eating disorder in terms of a group of understandable behaviors, thoughts, physiological reactions, and feelings, rather than seeing yourself as weak or crazy. Following assessment and starting treatment, sufferers describe a sense of relief at understanding their eating disorder. Understanding why you have an eating disorder

and what keeps it going can point out your strengths and how they can be dedicated to changing.

"They will force me to eat." There is no getting away from this – eating differently will be an important part of your recovery. However, your clinician should be aware that no one other than you can make this happen in a therapeutic way. Recovery from an eating disorder involves establishing a healthy relationship with food, and the clinician's job is to help you to change at a pace that you can manage. To be effective, this will be a pace where you are anxious about change (rather than being comfortable that no change can happen – that is not going to help you stop your eating problems), but not a pace that is so fast that you are paralyzed by anxiety. You will spend the early parts of treatment establishing goals around eating and food, developed in a collaborative fashion with your clinician. The only exception is where you are so ill that your life is threatened, when getting you safe has to be the priority.

"I will be locked up." The vast majority of eating disorders treatment is conducted on an outpatient, voluntary basis, and even in-patient treatment only involves detention on very rare occasions (usually where you are at imminent risk of death caused by the effects of malnutrition and where you are unwilling to engage in treatment voluntarily).

"My eating disorder will magically disappear and then what will I do?" Sometimes when sufferers seek further treatment, they fear that they will be "cured" by attending the assessment or beginning therapy. This thought can be frightening if the eating disorder is valuable in some way (e.g., it feels like a friend, or helps you to manage emotions). There can also be the fear that you will be nothing without the eating disorder. It is worth stressing that it is extremely unlikely that the eating disorder will just stop in this way, and if it did then there would probably be a recurrence very rapidly. Part of your treatment will involve addressing the aspects of the eating disorder that you found valuable, and exploring ways to achieve these aspects that do not center on eating, shape or weight.

"It is weak to get help." Sometimes people see it as weak or self-indulgent to seek help. This might be about your self-esteem, your upbringing, or the opinions of people around you. Just imagine a friend asking you if they deserved help. Would you describe their need as reflecting weakness or self-indulgence? Or would you tell them to get out there and get the help they need? Just treat yourself as well as you would treat them. You probably had no control over the circumstances that ended up with your developing an eating disorder, but you do have control over making changes to resolve it. However, that is not to downplay how tough this can feel. It takes courage and effort to get away from your problem, and you will have to put up with feeling scared by change before you can reap the benefits in the long term. Knowing when to seek help is a sign of strength, rather than reflecting weakness on your part.

"Treatment did not work last time – so what will be different?" Depending on your previous experiences with psychological treatments or other treatments for emotional problems (e.g., anti-depressant medication), you might be cautious

about seeking further help. If you are skeptical about whether treatment can really make a difference, it is worth keeping the following points in mind. First, the treatment you are offered might be delivered very differently this time around. Second, even if the treatment has the same label, treatments as a whole have developed. If your previous course of treatment was some years ago then the best options are likely to be more effective now. Third, your eating disorder or the reasons that you are seeking help might not be the same as last time (for example, you might previously have been anorexic and pushed into treatment by your family, which is likely to have a very different prognosis to that of someone seeking help under their own steam). Finally, and most importantly, the lack of success in your previous episode of treatment means that you have learned something valuable about that approach. You need to tell your clinician all about that previous treatment, to see if it means that there are better options this time round.

13

Starting the process of getting therapeutic help

This whole process begins with the decision to talk to a clinician, and then involves deciding what you will need to say to different people in the system who might support you, and what you can do to facilitate getting the right care for you.

Who should I talk to?

There are a variety of paths you could take, including support groups, treatment in a public healthcare system or private treatment. The way in which healthcare systems operate varies significantly from country to country so what follows is a general guide to what to expect and how to make sure that the treatment you get is the best possible for you (including being an active participant in your own treatment).

Your first point of contact will normally be your medical doctor. Hopefully, they know about your problem already, but if they do not then you need to be as frank as you can. Remember that their role is almost certainly to refer you to someone better placed to help you directly. Our experience (and the research base) says that simply turning up at your doctor's surgery and dropping hints is rarely effective. Your doctor will see many people each day with a variety of problems, so might not be well placed to spot your eating problem. However, if you can be honest and tell your doctor what is worrying you, then we find that medical doctors are usually very helpful in checking your physical health and referring you onwards. If you feel anxious, write down what you want to say, so that you remember to mention all of the things that are important to you. Check that you have mentioned all the behaviors and symptoms that we have talked about here in this book. It may be helpful to take someone with you for support. Let your doctor know that you have tried a self-help approach already. On the rare occasions where patients feel that they have not been listened to, we suggest trying a different doctor.

Following talking to your doctor, you might be referred for an assessment by a general mental health professional or by a specialist eating disorder clinician. This is likely to involve an assessment, resulting in a recommendation for treatment. To understand the applicability of those treatments to your individual problem, then we suggest that you read a document prepared for sufferers and carers, such as the relevant set of UK National Institute for Health and Clinical Excellence (NICE) guidelines (available online at http://www.nice.org.uk/guidance/index.jsp?action=download&o=29221).

Some doctors might want to refer you to a dietitian or someone else who is more qualified to help with the practical task of changing your eating than with the underlying emotional difficulties. While this may well be useful (especially if you are in the action phase of change), stick to your guns and emphasize your need for a more specialized assessment and treatment.

Preparing for your assessment

It is natural to experience some anxiety prior to your first appointment with a professional to discuss your eating disorder. You might feel shame or embarrassment about discussing your eating disorder behaviors or how you feel about yourself. If this is worrying you, remember that the professional whom you see is experienced in helping people with emotional difficulties, and is used to responding sensitively to difficult information. Many of our patients have reported a sense of relief at talking to someone who has an understanding of what they may be experiencing. Additionally, all professionals are bound by codes of conduct, which include the right to confidentiality. Do not be embarrassed to check on this point – you are entitled to be anxious and to be reassured. If you need support, take a family member or friend with you – they can sit in the waiting room while you attend your appointment, or they can come in if you feel that will be helpful. Again, jot down key points or questions, just in case your mind goes blank at a crucial moment.

One key point for while you are in the waiting room – you might well look around you and decide that you are nowhere near as ill as others who are there. Many clinicians will tell you that this is a very common theme for new patients. The only thing that we can say is that every patient there is probably thinking the same thing – that they are frauds, wasting everyone's time. Discuss this with your clinician, and they are very likely to tell you that everyone feels that way and that the key issue is whether the eating disorder is getting in the way of your life. Focus on that point, as you are probably not in a good place to make meaningful comparisons.

Your clinician will want to find out about you and your eating difficulties, in order to be able to recommend the best treatment for you. This means that you will be asked a number of questions, which might feel intrusive and will certainly be taxing, but the more information the clinician can gain, the better placed they will be to help you. It is likely you will be asked about the following topics:

1. Your current eating pattern (e.g., what you eat, when you eat, how much, etc.). It is really helpful if you take a diary of your past week's eating to the session, so that the clinician can get a clear picture of this (and you might find it hard to describe in the session).
2. Your current eating behaviors (e.g., bingeing, vomiting, use of laxatives, limiting of certain foods, etc.). Again, if you can note these in your diary, it will help matters along.
3. Your personal history, including your family and childhood experiences and the development of your eating problems (e.g., how your problems started, and how they got to where they are now). It can be helpful to try writing down a brief biography before you go along, to help you to get events in order and in perspective.
4. What your goals for treatment are.

Your clinician should also assess your physical state. At the very least, this will involve taking your height and weight. If there are other signs that the clinician is concerned about, then a wider medical screening will be important (e.g., taking bloods, arranging for a bone scan). The weighing is commonly the thing that scares new patients the most. Reflect on what you have read earlier in this book – there is no way past being weighed (or keeping diaries) if you want to have the best chance of getting well, and any clinician should be weighing you to ensure that you are safe, as a bare minimum. It is important to have an accurate and up-to-date weight for all patients. Although there is no way round this, your clinician will be aware that this might be anxiety provoking and will support you to tolerate the anxiety that you are feeling (e.g., "I will feel bad about myself"; "The clinician will see that I am fat and should not really be here").

How do I involve my carers (if I want to)?

How much you want to involve your carers (family or friends) is something you need to decide for yourself. If you feel you would like them to be involved, you can invite them to attend the clinic with you. Often, carers can be invited into the assessment towards the end of the appointment, if you choose. However, prior to inviting the carer into the room, the clinician should clarify with you what information you wish to share (e.g., confirmation of an eating disorder diagnosis; the plan for treatment; when your next appointment is). This also gives carers the opportunity to have any questions they might have answered. You might think that you know what all those questions are going to be, but sometimes your loved ones can surprise you with their insight and knowledge or, equally, the things they find harder to understand.

What treatment will I be offered?

Adults with eating disorders are likely to be offered individual outpatient treatment such as cognitive behavior therapy, cognitive analytic therapy, interpersonal therapy or psychodynamic therapy. Most commonly, this means attending for a one-hour appointment, on a weekly basis. These approaches have all been recognized as being potentially useful (National Institute for Health and Clinical Excellence, 2004).

The array of treatments available can be quite confusing, and not everything works for everybody. For individuals with bulimia or binge-type disorders, CBT has been shown to be the fastest-acting and most effective treatment. If your clinician suggests something else, then ask them to justify that choice. For individuals with a more anorexic type of illness, the findings are less definitive, but CBT remains a recommended treatment. The following are some important points to consider if you decide to engage in CBT.

There are some themes that are common across most outpatient therapies for eating disorders:

• If you are not sure whether you are ready to give up your eating disorder, it is likely that your clinician will work with you to explore your motivation to change.
• You will agree some individualized goals focused on staying safe, and working at a pace that feels manageable to you.
• You will be working at resolving your eating disorder and associated difficulties in your normal environment, meaning the changes are more likely to be relevant and long term.

If your clinician thinks that your eating disorder is more severe or you have tried outpatient treatment on several occasions, day-patient or in-patient treatment might be recommended. However, this is likely to be considered only when other options have been exhausted. The great majority of individuals will require outpatient treatment only.

Coping with waiting

Unfortunately, if you are offered treatment in a public health service, you are likely to be told that there is a waiting list for that treatment (unless your condition is urgent from a medical or psychiatric perspective – so be sure to be open about your symptoms). Such waiting can be frustrating, as you might feel that you need help immediately, having finally taken the step of seeking that help. You are likely to have to wait for weeks (more likely months) before your course of treatment can start. During this time, you may realize more and more how much your eating disorder is affecting your daily routine, relationships with others, and your mood. However, there are a number of sensible things that you can do while you wait, which can have a beneficial impact.

Sort out work and/or childcare. One of the things you should prioritize is talking to your boss or supervisor at your place of work about taking the necessary time off. Equally, if you are a parent with childcare responsibilities, take some time to arrange for your children to be looked after while you are attending your appointments. This can be a good time to get together with your carers to discuss matters. If the clinic is not able to see you outside your work hours, it is crucial that you make arrangements so that you can attend your weekly sessions. While some patients prefer not to tell work about the true reasons for taking time off to go for therapy, we have found that it is often best to be open and direct about this with your boss. Employers are usually support- ive if it is clear that you are actively doing something to improve your condition. Often a compromise can be arranged, which involves you making up the hours on a different day. If your company has an Occupational Health Department we recommend contacting them for support and advice about your rights.

When making these arrangements, think ahead. A typical course of CBT for bulimia nervosa involves about 20 weekly sessions, usually spread out over four to five months, while a typical course of CBT for anorexia nervosa involves about 40 weekly sessions, spread out over about a year. If you are clear with others about this being a limited time commitment, they are more likely to be support- ive than if you leave them wondering how long this will last.

Re-read the motivational, educational, and CBT elements of this book. Waiting for your first CBT appointment will give you the opportunity to familiarize yourself further with the self-help part of this book. In this way, you can prepare yourself for what is coming, and think about the kinds of questions you might want to ask. We have found that the individuals who do best in treatment are those who really "get into" the treatment, and one way of doing that is to keep reading and keep learning more about your eating disorder. Take some time to try some of the exercises. Keeping a food diary is probably one of the most useful tasks while you are waiting – as it will over time help you get a better understand- ing of your true eating pattern, and bringing the food records along to your first treatment session will allow your therapist to get a clear idea about them too.

Attending your first session of CBT

This may sound obvious, but a significant number of sufferers do not attend their first appointment. It is understandable that you will be nervous about meeting your clinician for the first time. After all, you will be talking to a complete stranger about problems that you may have had to keep a secret for a very long time. People can feel ashamed or embarrassed when telling their clinician about their difficulties, but as we have said before your clinician will be experienced in helping you understand and manage these feelings. The issue is not what has happened to you, but how your clinician can help you to make sense of it and plan treatment with you.

Sometimes, people assume that they are not worthy of treatment (e.g., "I'm not really that ill, they will think I'm a fraud") or that other people need treatment more (e.g., "I cannot take up their time – those other people in the waiting room clearly have much greater needs than I do"). This is not really something where you can decide, as you know little about other people's condi- tion, and you are probably not in a good position to judge your own condition.

Leave the decision about whether you merit treatment to your clinician, and focus on getting yourself there. In fact, we have never worked with anyone who was correct when they thought they didn't need treatment.

If you anticipate that you may be affected by any of these thoughts or feelings, plan ahead and devise a strategy to help. For example, take a friend or family member with you, or write some notes in advance to remind you why it is important to attend your appointment.

14

What to look for in a good CBT practitioner

Whether you are seeking a private clinician or one who is provided by a public health provider, what you need is a good practitioner, who is able to provide the therapy that will best address your problems. It is important to remember that clinicians vary substantially in quality and skills, and that how they label their work (whether it is CBT or another form of therapy) is not necessarily a good indicator of what they actually do in practice. On the assumption that you want the best therapy for your problem, then it is important that you know what to look for in a CBT practitioner (and know when to look elsewhere).

The therapeutic relationship

Perhaps the most important place to start is to consider the alliance between you and the clinician. Many sufferers value a warm, unpressured relationship with their clinician, where they feel understood but not pushed to make any change. Unfortunately, while such a friendly relationship is relatively easy to maintain, it is not likely to help you to change. Similarly, finding a clinician who is the same age, gender or ethnic group as you might feel relatively comfortable, but there is no evidence that it helps sufferers to recover when undertaking CBT. The therapeutic relationship in CBT needs to be both firm and empathic – your clinician needs to understand you, but needs to be willing to help you achieve change in your eating and other behaviors. It is important that you feel you can trust your therapist, and that she or he is interested in understanding you and your difficulties and wants to provide support for you as you change (rather than as you stay static).

Of course, this is very much a personal decision, but do not feel that you have to work with the first clinician whom you talk to. However, we recommend that if you ask to change, you do it in order to find a clinician who both understands you and will actively encourage you to change.

Accreditation/registration

One way to improve the likelihood that someone is suitably qualified to help you is to ask about their qualifications and their professional accreditation/registration. Qualified/registered clinicians typically have completed training in a core profession (e.g., clinical psychology, psychiatry, psychiatric nursing). Accredited clinicians will have completed some additional training in the relevant therapeutic approach (e.g., CBT). Ask your clinician about what qualifications they have and what professional body they are registered with, ensuring that they are qualified to specialize in their particular therapeutic approach. While accreditation and registration do not guarantee that the clinician is good enough, if your clinician cannot provide details of this sort, then you should be wary about their capacity to deliver evidence-based practice. You can ask your clinician for details of how to contact the relevant bodies, in order to verify their registration. Of course, it might feel difficult to question your clinician directly about such matters. Instead, you could try making a direct approach to the relevant professional bodies to check on the credentials of the clinician. This will vary from country to country. For example, in the UK, you could look up the name of the relevant clinician on the website of the Health Professions Council (http://hpc-portal.co.uk/online-register//) or the British Association for Behavioural and Cognitive Psychotherapies (http://cbtregisteruk.com/).

Willingness to talk about method

Asking questions about CBT in practice will enable you to get a feel for your clinician, and whether you want to work with this person. We have included examples of very sensible questions that we have been asked, and some answers that we would expect any good CBT clinician to be able to provide. If your clinician does not give you similar answers, then you might ask them to clarify, and even to explain why their approach is not similar to what we have outlined here. Be clear that you expect high-quality therapy, and that you are aware of the basics of what makes up such a therapy:

Can you tell me a bit about CBT? This is a critical question. Can your clinician explain how CBT differs from other therapies that you might have encountered? Look for an answer such as:

> CBT is a type of therapy that focuses mostly on the present and the future, although at times we may explore the past to understand how things may be affecting you in the "here and now". In a nutshell, CBT involves understanding the link between our thoughts, our feelings, our biology, and our behaviors. By understanding those connections, we can begin to change our thoughts and manage our feelings better. In turn, we can stop unhelpful patterns of behavior that have been reinforcing the original negative thoughts and feelings. As well as eating disorders, CBT is used to help people with depression, anxiety, phobias and obsessive–compulsive disorder.

Your clinician might illustrate the links between your thoughts, feelings, biology, and behaviours using the "hot cross bun" that we outlined above. This is usually a good sign that the clinician sees it as important to explain things to you clearly, even at this early stage.

How does CBT help people with eating disorders? You should hope that your clinician will give you an answer such as:

> CBT for eating disorders focuses initially primarily on what is keeping your eating disorder going. First, we will work on regularizing your eating and addressing any problem behaviors such as vomiting, excessive exercise or bingeing. Developing out of that, we will address the thoughts and feelings you have about your eating and more generally, yourself as a person. This may include working on your body image, if appropriate. The final stage involves preparing for the ending of therapy and planning for the future. If you are underweight, we will also work on helping you to reach a healthy weight.

Remember that evidence-based approaches to eating disorders start with behavioral change – not just with talking about change.

What do I need to do? Look for an answer such as:

> CBT is a 168-hour-a-week therapy – that means we will meet for one hour a week and then you need to put the skills and strategies you learn in the session into practice throughout the rest of the week. That includes homework tasks. CBT is an "active" treatment, which means you will be working hard to implement changes, and you will need to prioritize your treatment to get the best results. CBT is a collaborative therapy – that means you and I will be working *together* to address your difficulties. It is hard work, and unfortunately there is no magic wand. However, we do know that if people do work hard, they are likely to see results.

How many sessions will I need, and do I have to come every week? Many sufferers hope that treatment is something that they can pick up and put down. We would hope that your clinician would stress that this is not possible:

> These skills are really hard to learn, and you will need to have lots of practice. Particularly at the beginning of treatment, it is essential to meet on a weekly basis. Although everybody is different, as a rule of thumb, individuals with bulimia usually need 20 sessions and those with anorexia might need approximately 40 sessions.

Some clinicians might even suggest meeting twice weekly for the first week or so, in order to help you develop your skill base. However, weekly meetings should be enough after that time period, as long as you are doing all the work that is recommended.

Will this treatment make me better? Most clinicians will tell you that their therapeutic approach will be of benefit. If your clinician cannot tell you about the research base, then you need to consider how up-to-date they are. Look for an answer that is honest, such as:

> As long as you are not significantly underweight (in the anorexic range) and you do all the work of CBT, then your chances of recovering fully and avoiding relapse are about

50%. Even if you do not recover fully, you have a good chance of a significant reduction in the symptoms that are impairing your life. This is a better outcome (and a faster one) than any other psychological therapy. If your weight is in the anorexic range, your chances of recovery are nearer to 30–35 %, as long as you do all the work. Again, this is a better outcome than you can expect from other therapies.

Even better, a reflective CBT clinician will be able to tell you *their* local therapeutic outcomes. How well they have done with one or more patients in a similar position to yourself. A clinician who reflects on their work in this way is much more likely to be improving their practice.

Do I have to be weighed/keep food diaries/have blood taken/come to all the sessions/ change my eating? These are very common questions, all of which are likely to reflect your anxiety about the risks of finding out how serious your problem is and your fears of change. These are all "non-negotiables" – things that have to happen if CBT is to be effective. Therefore, your clinician should be saying a firm: "Yes – all these are needed for your safety and for you to have the best chance of recovering." If you say "no" to any of these, then your clinician should be reminding you that you are not doing CBT, and that your chances of recovery are consequently lower. Indeed, if you are refusing to allow your medical condition to be monitored, your clinician might need to say that there is no point continuing in this way, as all that you are doing is increasing your physical risk. It might be necessary to stop therapy in order to ensure that your physical safety is focused on.

Willingness to talk about the process of therapy

Your clinician should be willing to talk to you about the concerns that come up in the process of therapy, as many sufferers experience them:
- "I'm not ready."
- "It's getting harder not easier."
- "I don't think I'll ever get better."
- "My drinking or drugs are getting in the way."

How to overcome these issues varies so much from case to case, so it is not possible to address them properly here. The point is that you should be able to raise them with your clinician and have meaningful discussions about how to get past them. If your clinician dismisses such worries on your part, then they are not taking you seriously. However, if your clinician lets those concerns take over to the point where therapy stops, then they are not taking your recovery seriously.

15

The role of carers in the transition to more formal help

As we have already illustrated throughout this book, carers can help in a wide variety of ways, from providing emotional support to offering very real practical help in completing tasks. As long as such help is negotiated with the sufferer and is offered flexibly according to the situation, then it can be of help.

What can I do to help my loved one get help?

While the level of emotional support you give is likely to be unaffected (unless your loved one is anxious about change and needs to be able to talk about it), the transition into more formal help means that you and the sufferer will need to discuss how the practical help that you can offer will need to change. In particular, it is worth discussing the following topics:

- accompanying your loved one to the family physician to get a referral
- ensuring that your loved one does the basics of looking after their physical health (e.g., getting blood tests done, as recommended by clinicians)
- coming to the assessment (even if it is only to be there in the waiting area when they emerge)
- giving the sufferer the chance to reflect on the session
- helping with homework practice
- changing how you shop, store food, eat meals, etc. to help your loved one to live more normally around food
- whether your loved one is changing, for better or worse (e.g., "Well, I know you think that your eating is much better now, but it really has a long way to go before you are eating like the rest of us"; "You know, when I say that you look healthier, I really mean that – not that you look fat")

Of course, all this is (probably) new to you, and you might be thinking "Who is there to support me as I go through this difficult time?" We recommend the following:

- Talk to your loved one's clinician. This will depend on your loved one being happy about you talking to the clinician, and the discussion might be relatively generalized (to avoid problems of confidentiality), but the advice and explanation of the therapy can be invaluable. Some eating disorder services will run carer support groups where you can meet other families and hear from each other about ways of supporting both the individual and yourselves.

- Find out about local family support groups, helplines and websites (see Appendix 1). Try them and see if they are helpful for you (particularly in helping you understand your loved one's behavior and emotions, and their effect on you).
- Share your concerns with your loved one, in a non-blaming way. Be honest about your fears for their mental and physical health, but try to ensure that this is not such an emotive experience that neither of you feels safe returning to the topic.
- Read more about the emotional and practical skills that you need to cope with your loved one's needs. As we have mentioned above, an excellent resource is the book on this subject by Treasure, Smith, and Crane (2007) (see the reference list at the back of this book).
- If you are asked to participate in the therapy (e.g., family work, couples work), then give it a go. This may feel anxiety-provoking. However, do remember that many clinicians are concerned with carers as a resource to help the sufferer change, rather than looking to blame you for the problem.

We recommend accepting help when it is offered as change is very difficult and we all need people on our side. The main issue is to be clear in your own mind about what might be helpful, and to think about what is the best way to communicate this to your loved one.

So why is it so hard to help my loved one?

It is not always easy to provide the care and support that you would like to during this phase. Sometimes that is because of the sufferer's experiences and fears; other times it is because of your own reactions and expectations. The following are some common reasons why it can be hard to help your loved one.

Investing everything in treatment. It can be a huge sense of relief for you when your loved one begins formal treatment. This is not surprising, given how long you have all lived with the eating disorder. It can be difficult for the sufferer if you see this as *the* opportunity for them to get better, and if you get anxious that the sufferer should not waste this chance. It is important to remember this is only the beginning of another journey for the sufferer, and it is perfectly normal for them to struggle at times through this journey. Adjusting your support accordingly means the sufferer has more likelihood of continuing successfully with the journey.

Recovery is not immediate. Recovery from an eating disorder takes a significant amount of time. You will need to discuss the process of therapy with the sufferer, rather than continually asking whether they are better now. If the sufferer cannot tell you about the bad times in treatment because they feel that they are failing your expectations, then you cannot help just when they need it most.

Needing to accept that you cannot know everything. The clinician cannot discuss your loved one with you without their permission. If they could, then you would probably find that your loved one was not completely honest with the clinician. Just remember that it is perfectly normal for other people to keep things to themselves at some level, so do not treat this as a problem. You should simply remember that the clinician will take action if they consider that your loved one is in danger of physical harm.

Needing to find a new role for you. As a significant amount of your time has probably been given to the sufferer, it will be important to be able to let go when the sufferer is ready to move forward as she or he makes progress in treatment. This might mean reflecting upon your own behavior and finding other activities to fill your time.

Letting go of the eating disorder

It can be difficult to let go of your eating disorder, for a number of different reasons. Indeed, many people have their eating disorder for some time before they decide to seek help or to make changes. The process of recovering from an eating disorder can also take a number of years. Some people feel "stuck" at the age at which they developed their eating disorder, and your eating disorder might mean that you missed out on things such as relationships, friends, a career or living independently. Your eating disorder might have meant that you haven't had to be an adult or make decisions about your life. Alternatively, you might have done these things, but always with your eating disorder in the background, acting as a support or "safety net." Given all this, you might be wondering what life would be like without your eating disorder.

And then there are those around you. One of the issues that sufferers often find difficult is that family and friends do not understand what you perceive to be the "good" things about your eating disorder. This can mean that while they are very pleased that you are working to recover from your eating disorder, they might overlook some of your worries. Recovering from your eating disorder means that you will have to face your fears and take risks, just like everybody else does, but that you might also be at risk of relapsing. This section is about letting go of your eating disorder, and working to stay free of your eating disorder.

Some sufferers reading this book will have been able to make some but not all of the changes they need to. However far you have progressed, it is still important to read this chapter, to help you consolidate the changes you have made and to begin to explore the steps you may need to take to continue with your journey.

For carers, large parts of this book have focused on the changes that the individual with the eating disorder needs to make. However, this section also reflects on the changes that you might need to make as your partner, child, parent or friend moves towards recovery.

16

The journey of recovery

Sufferers tend to have a "black or white" thinking style. We have known many people who come to treatment expecting to be "cured" by the end, or alternatively, not to finish treatment until they are completely free of their eating disorder. We find that it is easier to think of your recovery from your eating disorder as a journey. Remember the "Coast of South America" analogy in Chapter 7. By the time you are reading the current chapter, it is likely that you have undertaken a large proportion of your journey. You have probably experienced a number of ups and downs – times when you were pleased to see the changes and progress you made and times when you felt hopeless and overwhelmed. Just as the experience of the trek will give the trekker skills and confidence in their own ability, your experience will have highlighted your skills and the steps you have taken in your recovery journey. We hope that this has given you the confidence to continue your journey independently.

Take the next few minutes to think about the journey you have made. What was life like before you decided to address your eating disorder? What were your typical thoughts and feelings? If you were using eating disorder behaviors such as bingeing, vomiting or excessive exercise, how often were these happening? How were your relationships? How were your concentration and your ability to do and enjoy the things you wanted to do? How do you feel physically now compared to before? It is likely that you may have made some significant changes, although you may have forgotten or got used to just how far you have come. It is also possible that some of your eating disorder behaviors and attitudes are still around – although less intense – and that you fear you will relapse. These are all very normal concerns, and are to be expected at this stage. The reality is that you will not suddenly get better – more that you will change over time. You will gradually notice a decrease in the frequency and intensity of your eating disorder thoughts and feelings, until one day you will have to think hard to remember the last time you had such thoughts or feelings. The smoking analogy below might illustrate the process.

The smoking analogy

Imagine you are a smoker. You have smoked for a number of years and are gradually becoming aware that the cons outweigh the pros. You know that smoking is bad for your health and is affecting your fitness, and you are fed up of having to stand outside the bar in the cold in order to have a cigarette. You decide to give up. You ask your friends and partner to support you. You decide that, for the time being, you need to avoid "risky" situations, such as going out with the other smokers at work. You work at cutting down, and then stopping completely. At first, you find that all you can think about is cigarettes and how much you are craving them. There are times when you may have to have a cigarette. After a while, you notice the cravings are less intense and there are actually times when you are not thinking about a cigarette. You remain aware that you need to be careful not to go back to smoking. Every now and again, you get an urge to smoke but you are able to control it. Time continues to pass until one day you realize that you can't remember the last time you thought about having a cigarette.

Are there healthier alternatives to my eating disorder behaviors?

As we have said before, there may be some parts of your eating disorder that feel harder to let go of, such as wanting to remain underweight or continuing to use binge-eating as a treat or to block negative emotions. Look back to Chapter 5, where you listed the pros and cons of your eating disorder. Are the pros of your eating disorder still relevant? If they are, is there another way you can achieve that function without using your eating disorder? A table like the one below would help (see Table 16.1).

Table 16.1

Pros of my eating disorder (from Chapter 5)	Is this still important to me now?	Is there another way I can meet this need?

Who am I if I do not have my eating disorder?

As we said earlier, you may have had your eating disorder for a number of years, perhaps since childhood. Particularly for those who suffer from anorexia, your illness might have become tangled up with your identity – who you believe you are as a person. Your eating disorder or being very underweight might have made you feel special or different. It can be hard to imagine who you would be or what you would do if you didn't have your anorexia. You might worry about how your family and friends will perceive you. Feeling that your eating disorder is part of your identity indicates that your eating disorder is fairly entrenched, and you might feel that you need further professional help for you to explore this issue of your identity, and to enable further change. This is more about who you are than getting away from your eating disorder, but it is important in meaning that you can leave the eating disorder behind.

For now, try the following exercise to build up a picture of who you are and who you might like to be:
• First, make a list of all your likes and dislikes. You could include favorite colors, smells, books, or films, and places you've been to.
• Now make a list of all the activities or experiences you enjoy (or used to enjoy).
• Add a list of qualities or characteristics that you possess or used to possess before your illness (e.g., kindness, hot-headedness, or a sense of humor). If you feel you can, ask friends and family what they might add to this list. Come back to it and add to it whenever you think of something new.

Now look at your lists – particularly the third one. How does your eating disorder fit with the items on the list? Does your eating disorder help you to be that person, or does it get in the way of being you? In our experience, when former sufferers try this exercise, they are usually surprised by how many characteristics appear on the list and how the eating disorder had narrowed their identity.

What if I can't make all the changes now?

Many of you reading this will have been able to make positive changes regarding your eating and your thoughts about your shape and weight. However, for some sufferers, this approach will not have been sufficient to help you recover fully. This might be because of a range of factors about you, other people, and the world (e.g., motivation to change, remaining in a difficult home environment, stress at work). We have talked about internal factors (such as motivation and anxiety about change) in earlier chapters, and you might need to revisit those chapters to decide if you really cannot make the changes now or if you are trying to stay "a bit anorexic" (see below), but it is worth considering how the external world is impacting on you, and what you might be able to do about this.

It is important to review the *function* of the eating disorder and the external influences. For some individuals, the function of an eating disorder will be to manage intolerable distress and/or to achieve some degree of control in an otherwise uncontrollable situation. If you are in an abusive relationship or a victim of domestic violence, you may need to find a way out of that situation before you are able to make significant changes in your eating disorder. You may feel you need your eating disorder just to survive day to day. Similarly, remaining in a "toxic" environment – such as a critical family environment, an environment where there is a heavy emphasis on weight and dieting, or a career or hobby that promotes thinness (e.g., modeling, ballet, athletics) is likely to make recovery difficult. You need to take some time to think about whether you will be able to make the changes you want to in your current situation, or whether you need to start planning now for an eventual "escape route."

Another possibility is that you have considered the time and effort necessary to allow you to recover, and decided that those costs are too high, given the other priorities in your life at present. Competing demands are increasingly common as life gets busier, and you may need to come back to therapy when you have the space in your life. However, before you let yourself give up on change because of those other priorities and goals (e.g., workload, raising children), ask yourself whether the impact of your eating disorder on your life is making it easier or harder to achieve those goals. Many sufferers find that the effects of starvation and other eating behaviors on their capacity to think and deal with their emotional states makes it harder to achieve the very things they are trying to prioritize. The way out of this vicious cycle is to work on your eating disorder, rather than on other things.

Can I stay "a bit anorexic/bulimic"?

Many sufferers hope they will be able to get rid of the "bad" or unwanted parts of their eating disorder (e.g., bingeing or vomiting) while hanging onto the "good" bits (especially low weight). Although this sounds ideal in theory, in reality it is impossible. An eating disorder consists of a number of vicious cycles based on physiological and psychological factors. If you leave part of the eating disorder intact, it is likely that the vicious cycle will be maintained. For example, maintaining a low weight or restrictive eating pattern puts you at risk of bingeing and keeps you preoccupied with thoughts of control over eating, shape, and weight.

Think about other times that you have tried to stop your eating disorder without addressing all the problem behaviors. Was it successful? That seems unlikely, given that you are reading this book. We are not suggesting that the partial changes you have made already are not important – just being honest about the fact that this is unlikely to be enough. You cannot be "a bit anorexic" or "a bit bulimic." In our experience, trying to remain "part eating disordered" is impossible, and will mean that you continue to be negatively affected by your eating disorder.

What if the eating disorder comes back?

The need to be perfect and an all-or-nothing thinking style often mean that when something goes wrong, eating disorder sufferers think to themselves "That's it... I'm back to square one, I'm never going to get better, I should give up now!" In fact, for everybody, mistakes are an essential part of the learning process. Mistakes enable us to develop a more robust knowledge and understanding, and give us confidence to cope when things are not going smoothly. Understanding why things have gone wrong makes it far more likely that we will manage more successfully in the future. Imagine if you were teaching a friend, or a child, how to do something new (e.g., swimming, knitting, or learning a new language). Would you expect them to get it perfect first time? In fact, you would be prepared for mistakes and stumbling blocks. We guess you would offer encouragement, rather than the harsh words you might save for yourself.

It is very common to worry that any slip is a relapse or even a complete collapse. What you need to learn now is that a slip is a lapse, which you can recover from. A lapse only becomes a relapse or a collapse if you give up and respond to it by ignoring everything that you have learned in your CBT. In face-to-face CBT, clinicians are usually very understanding if the person has gone back to using some of their old behaviors (e.g., had a binge), and your therapist would typically encourage you to use the lapse as a sign that you need to get back to using your CBT skills (e.g., "I realized that I had let my snacks slip a bit, so I put them back in and I did not binge again"). You need to be clear about the meanings of the three terms (lapse, relapse, and collapse) and remember that the difference depends on how you react to the early signs (the lapse).

• *Lapse.* This term describes what happens when there is a single, isolated slip while you are actively working on learning and implementing a skill. For example, you might have managed to stop bingeing or vomiting for two weeks, but then find these behaviors reoccurring in the third week. The trigger might be an argument with your partner or eating in a restaurant, or you might be puzzled as to how the slip occurred. The key skill is to identify your trigger situations and to make the changes that will get you back on track. You can learn to identify the "early warning signs," which are likely to be similar to the stressors that you had before starting treatment (e.g., hunger, emotions, social situations). Remember how you learned to identify and deal with these triggers in CBT, and start looking for them as soon as you get the urge to use your old behaviors. Then you will be able to use the skills that you learned to cope with them (e.g., eat more regularly, avoid impossible social situations in favor of more positive experiences, allow yourself to experience your emotions as motivators for change, rather than as terrifying experiences). That way, you can avoid a single, isolated slip (a lapse) becoming a repeated pattern (a relapse).

• *Relapse.* This term describes a series of slips, resulting in you no longer applying the skills you have learned. This can happen during treatment, but more often happens in the first few weeks after finishing treatment. When this happens, it is important not to panic and assume that a return to your illness is inevitable (a collapse). As with a single slip, be honest with yourself if you have let yourself off the hook on the core tasks of healthy eating (e.g., eating enough food and on a regular basis; not using food to deal with emotions) and reinstate what you have learned. Use relapse prevention work (see the next chapter) to identify what you need to do to get back on track. Remember that the crux of CBT is becoming your own therapist, and if you start re-applying the tools (see below) you should find it relatively easy to get yourself back on track. This will help you to avoid a collapse.

• *Collapse.* This occurs when a lapse becomes a relapse, and you are unable to stem the problem in how you are coping with food and the world. Eventually you find that many of your old difficulties have re-emerged – maybe losing weight, maybe bingeing and purging, maybe exercising excessively – and it is hard to recall the knowledge and skills gained in therapy. This is a collapse. It is not an uncommon occurrence, and can explain why some people need more than one go at an effective, evidence-based therapy such as CBT. Therapy can only be effective when you keep integrating the lessons of CBT into everyday life throughout your treatment (e.g., eating normally for so long that it becomes second nature). Fortunately, the available evidence shows that relapse rates are relatively low with CBT (assuming it is done properly), compared with other therapies. Collapse is more likely if you are hanging on to part of your eating disorder (e.g., wanting to be very thin). When collapse occurs, it can be easy to be disheartened. It is likely that you will need to re-start some of the tasks of therapy you learned at the beginning. However, even now you can learn the importance of keeping up the tasks of CBT, so that when you have your eating and thinking back to normal again you will know what to do to avoid another collapse in the future.

It is important to remember that every relapse begins with a few isolated lapses, and every collapse begins with a relapse. If you want to stay well, then it is vitally important to:

1. Get as well as you can in the first place (not just get a bit better and hope the rest will follow).
2. Recognize the early signs of any return to your eating disorder (re-emerging old patterns of either thinking or eating).
3. Respond to those early signs by making active changes to your eating, and challenging and testing your beliefs about your eating and your body.

To ensure that you can stop yourself from letting go of all control, it is important to recognize what you have learned and the skills that you now have for keeping your eating normal and healthy. Right now, when you are feeling more in charge, let us consider what you have in your therapy "toolbox" that can help you to stay healthy. Thinking about your toolbox when your eating has improved and you are feeling more healthy is much more effective than waiting until there is a crisis (similar to preparing a flashcard when you do not need it at that moment, but preparing for when you do).

Table 16.2 My toolbox

Useful strategies	Page number in this book	Why is this important? When is it useful?
Sticking to regular, balanced meals and snacks	64–70	
Completing a food diary	60–61	
Developing alternative coping strategies	40–41	
Revisiting the psychoeducation	53–56	
Reviewing my goals (short, medium, and long term)	38–40	
Reviewing motivation work	23–32	
Talking to a supportive friend/family member	37–38	
Thought records	72–73	
Positive data log	73–75	
Flashcard	75	
Exposure to anxiety	78–79, 89	
Behavioral experiments	79–82, 89	
Surveys	90–91	
Other strategies	–	

What's in your toolbox?

The strategies you have learned in this book are like the tools in a toolbox. If we need to do some work around the house, we get out our toolbox. We evaluate what we need to do, and select the tool that we believe to be best for the job. Sometimes, we choose the right tool first time. On other occasions, the job will turn out to be different from what we expected and we will have to switch tools (e.g., swap the spanner for some pliers). As you continue after this book, you will have your toolbox of strategies to help you negotiate problems – eating-related or otherwise. It might be that as you identify a difficulty, the first strategy you choose does not accomplish all you need. However, as you have learned here, you should not give up when that happens. Now that you know why that first tool was not the right one, you are in a better place to go back to your toolbox to select another tool, until the difficulty is resolved. (With acknowledgement to our colleague, Katie Russell.)

Listed above in "My toolbox" (Table 16.2) are some of the strategies and skills that you have developed over the course of this book, and where you will find them in the book. Make sure you add others that you have discovered, and make notes about when and why a strategy is most useful for you.

So, having reviewed your tools, it is time to think about how to use them to achieve "relapse prevention" – strategies to help you deal with unforeseen events and changes that might lead you to start using your eating behaviors again.

17

Relapse prevention

In terms of the "Coast of South America" analogy (Chapter 7), you are now reaching Brazil. You have done the hard work, including putting up with the feeling that you are going the wrong way (south rather than east), and you have seen real change in your eating disorder. You might even be feeling cautious optimism about the future. In terms of motivational state, you are in "maintenance" (Chapter 5). This state can be challenging, because you have to maintain your changes alongside dealing with other life difficulties that crop up, but without using your previous strategy (your eating disorder) to cope. If you don't practice what you have learned, next time you want to use your new skills you will find they are rusty.

Forewarned is forearmed

It may seem that we are being unduly negative in considering the possibility of relapse. However, forewarned is forearmed. We hope that things go smoothly for you, but life can be unpredictable. There can be many triggers to relapse, including both internal events (low mood, concerns about body image, need to feel in control) and external events (relationship breakdown, divorce, bereavement, other change in circumstances). Treatment does not render you invulnerable to such triggers (anyone could be affected by these, whether or not they have had an eating disorder), but should have made you aware of them and equipped you with protective strategies. In times of stress, you might find that the need to control your eating, shape, and weight become prominent in your mind again. Relapse prevention is about your dealing with those stressors in an adaptive way, rather than going back to your old ways.

The exercises below aim to assist you in reflecting over your progress and in developing a "relapse prevention plan." First, you need to identify your own, personal set of warning signs and risky situations. Then you need a structured reminder of what worked for you – the therapy blueprint.

Exercise 1: Warning signs and risky situations

Hindsight is a wonderful thing but no real help on its own. The next best thing is to be forewarned. What are your warning signs that you might be lapsing, and what are the risky situations for you? If you have experienced relapse before, what could you learn from that? Write down these early warning signs and risky situations for yourself on a flashcard.

Katy developed the following flashcard to remind her of her warning signs and risky situations:
- Beginning to skip meals and avoid carbohydrates
- Counting kilocalories
- Starting to body-check again and weighing myself frequently
- Avoiding friends and/or dating because of concerns about my appearance
- Noticing a return of urges to binge, purge or use laxatives again
- Planning for holidays by focusing on whether I am thin enough
- Starting a new job, where I am worried about how other people will see me

---

Exercise 2: Developing your therapy blueprint

The therapy blueprint is the core element of your relapse prevention. It is a summary of all the work you have undertaken in recent months, and what has worked for you as an individual. When you have completed CBT, read the blueprint on a weekly basis until it feels like second nature to think and act that way. The blueprint is your personal "therapy for me" book. The key steps in preparing the blueprint are:
- *identify your previous pattern of thoughts, feelings, behaviors, and physical state, so that you can see how far you have come with therapy*
- *draw out or write down an account of how you developed your eating disorder, and what kept it going for so long*
- *identify your personal risk factors that may lead to a return of your eating disorder*
- *write an account of what your CBT has done to help you (alternative strategies for coping)*

Appendix 20 gives you your own therapy blueprint sheet, so that you can complete this when you have got to the end of your self-help program. Make sure that you complete this when you are eating normally and feeling healthy again, so that you can remind yourself of how far you have come.

Jenny's therapy blueprint looked like this:

Jenny's therapy blueprint

Identify your previous pattern of thoughts, feelings, behaviors, and physical state: *Before starting this treatment program, I was in a bad way physically. I was significantly underweight, my periods had stopped and I often felt cold and tired. I was unable to concentrate properly at work. My thoughts were consumed by my weight and what I was going to eat that day. I felt sad, anxious, and lonely. My thoughts about myself were: "I'm a failure" and "Being thin is the only way to stay in control and succeed." I followed a restrictive diet, spent hours exercising in the gym, had to have "low fat" or "diet" products, and couldn't do anything nice like go to a restaurant or have a spontaneous drink with friends.*

Write down an account of how you developed your eating disorder, and what kept it going for so long:

My anorexia developed when I was about 18, when my parents were divorcing and I was stressed about exams. I worried that I was somehow to blame for my parents split. Everything felt very out of control and I worried about failing my exams. It seemed that losing weight was the only thing that I was good at and gave me a sense of feeling in control. I went into hospital and gained weight but didn't change my thinking so when I came out I lost the weight again. However, I was so scared of going back into hospital again that I managed to control how much weight I lost. I found myself increasingly caught in rigid routines that I could not change. Life got more lonely and isolated and I worried what it would be like without the anorexia to support me. It felt too scary to change things in case my weight and everything else went out of control.

Identify your risk factors for returning to your eating disorder:
• *Feeling overwhelmed at work.*
• *Comments about my appearance now that I have reached a healthy weight for the first time in years.*
• *Interpersonal difficulties with family or friends.*
• *Difficulties in my new relationship.*

Write an account of what your CBT has done to help you (alternative strategies for coping):

CBT has helped me understand how I was using my anorexia to stay in control, both of my body and my feelings. Being thin enabled me to feel successful (even though it doesn't make a difference really!) particularly if I felt overwhelmed at work. However, I began to realize the cons of my anorexia – the physical impact, exhaustion from constant striving, the loneliness, and problems with fertility. I realized I was missing out on life! I have learnt that being a healthy weight isn't as scary or impossible as I thought it would be. I still have "bad" days but am gradually accepting my new shape. My weight has stabilized and not shot up, as I feared it would. I definitely like that I have more energy and people have commented that I seem happier. Actually relaxing my control of my eating has meant that I am more in control of my eating. Talking to friends and family has definitely helped. Instead of dwelling on things, I either write them down or discuss with a friend – this helps me take a broader perspective – and I can often challenge the worry or find a solution. From time to time I look through my notebook, which reminds me how far I have come and what I need to keep doing.

Planning for the future – getting your life back

You already knew that having an eating disorder takes up a lot of time – time spent worrying about calories or your appearance, "hiding your secret", exercising, or visiting multiple supermarkets to get the "right" food. It has probably stopped you doing things, such as eating in restaurants or spending time with friends. You might have been so exhausted that you have had very little energy left to do anything else. Having an eating disorder means your life can get very "narrow" – hobbies, friends, and family can be neglected or forgotten about. This might all have happened so subtly that you have not been aware of it until now. Your eating disorder has probably led to you "putting things on hold." Future planning will also have been affected. Maybe you were avoiding intimate relationships, or maybe your self-esteem was low, so you felt held back in life. Maybe you wanted to change career but didn't feel able to. Giving up an eating disorder can leave a void that makes it more likely you will relapse. Therefore, it can be helpful to devise some goals for what you want over the next few months, just as you did at the start of this book.

Use the grid below (Table 17.1) to start planning goals for the short, medium and long term. These might include some of the goals that you had before your eating disorder began. It will probably include some of the goals that you had or developed while you had your eating disorder, or even ones that became far more important as a result of seeing what your eating disorder took away from you (e.g., having a family). However, it is also likely that you will find new goals. These can be changed as you go along – the freedom of not having an eating disorder means that you are not obliged to stick rigidly to what you have always done. The real point is that you are now free to do as others do – to set realistic, achievable goals for your life, to find out if they are right for you, and to change them as you go along.

Review sessions

Whether you are in therapy with a clinician or using a self-help approach, it is helpful to continue with personal therapy sessions once formal therapy is over.

Table 17.1 My goals

	Goals for the short term (1–6 months)	Goals for the medium term (6–12 months)	Goals for the long term (12 months +)
My eating disorder			
My friends			
My family			
My relationships			
My hobbies/things I enjoy			
My work/study			
Other			

By this, we mean setting aside a time, ideally once a week, to reflect on the past week and to plan for upcoming weeks. Plan out an agenda, including:
- How has my eating been?
- Have I used any eating disorder behaviors?
- What am I not doing that would help me to stay free of my eating disorder?
- Am I achieving my goals?

Be honest with yourself, and you have a much better chance of achieving your long-term goals. Talking about this process with your loved ones can help enormously, if you feel ready to share your goals with them. They can help you to stay on track far better if they are part of your personal therapy sessions.

A word of warning: the risks of weight loss

It is common for ex-sufferers to want to lose weight. It is important to consider whether that is viable for you, or whether it is likely to tip you back into the eating disorder. It is not possible to tell you the right weight for you, but if you have recovered (e.g., your periods are back, you are not bingeing or vomiting, you can eat a wide range of foods without panic, you are not judging yourself in terms of your appearance) at your current weight, then that is a weight that you can maintain. Unless you are objectively overweight (say a body mass index of 25 or above – see Section 3, p. 52 for how to work this out), then weight loss might be a risky target. A general rule of thumb is that your body is the best indicator of whether you can lose weight. If weight loss makes you tip into your old ways of thinking or behaving, then you are doing it too much or too fast. If you slow it down and you still tip into your old ways, then you should probably try to stay at your current weight. Your body is unlikely to be convinced by "But I *should* be lighter."

If you are objectively overweight and you want to lose weight for health reasons, then you will find that fast weight loss is not sustainable. Many people decide that they want to diet, but start on a starvation level (e.g., 1000 kcal for a woman). Such a reduction in intake is not sustainable without pushing you back towards eating problems (either overeating because you are ravenous, or getting you back into thinking in an anorexic style). We advise that you aim to reduce your diet by 200–400 kcal per day, but definitely no more than 500 kcal per day. The weight loss might feel disappointingly slow, but is sustainable in the long term. In short, do you want to return to yo-yo dieting where the best that you achieve is to stay at your current level of overweight (but where you are more likely to see your weight gradually drift up), or do you want slow, maintained progress? Our recommendation might only cause you to lose a kilogram every month or so, but if you maintain that for a couple of years then you can be substantially lighter, healthier, and without a recurrence of symptoms.

If you are losing weight, then every few months we recommend that you stop trying to lose, and focus for a month on a second skill – keeping your weight stable. It is really important to remember that you have two skills to learn – weight loss (which most eating disorder sufferers are very good at) and weight stability (which most sufferers are quite poor at). You need that second skill so that you can stop focusing on your weight when you get to a safer, healthy level. Most importantly (and like anyone else who is overweight), ensure that you take medical advice about your health status if you are overweight and when you are learning to lose weight, and combine dietary reduction with moderate exercise.

Dealing with other issues

We have talked earlier about other difficulties that often go hand in hand with an eating disorder – for example, depression, anxiety or obsessive–compulsive disorder. For most people, these difficulties improve significantly as their eating disorder improves. Others might need a more structured intervention. For example, you might have experienced events that you feel you need to continue to work on (e.g., sexual abuse, rape, divorce, bereavement). It is also possible that you will have pre-existing problems that need to be addressed (e.g., social anxiety, panic, low self-esteem). Your family physician or eating disorder clinician can help you to find a suitable place for this, even if they cannot work on those issues with you personally. There are also good self-help books for each of these. We have listed some of the most useful under 'further reading' in the References section at the back of this book.

18

Have I done myself permanent damage?

It is very common for eating disorder sufferers to worry about this. There is no doubt that starving, bingeing, vomiting, taking laxatives, and diet pills each have short-term effects. However, relatively few patients who have recovered from an eating disorder have done themselves long-term damage. If you are concerned about this, then talk to your family doctor about your concerns, and ask for a physical check-up.

There are two areas where it is particularly important that you are informed, as these are recurrent topics of concern among recovering sufferers – bone structure and fertility.

Bone structure

If you have been underweight with your periods absent for two or more years, there is a chance that your bone structure will have been weakened (osteopenia, or the more severe osteoporosis). In essence, your bones have a honeycomb structure (to keep them light but strong). Long-term low weight means that the holes in the honeycomb are getting larger, weakening their structure. A common interpretation is that anorexics can have a skeleton that is similar in its weakness to that of a much older person. In severe and chronic cases, adolescent sufferers can fail to develop to their full potential height, and adult sufferers can lose height. The amount of bone loss varies considerably from person to person, so the only way of finding out is to ask your doctor to carry out a bone scan (dexa scan), and to repeat this every couple of years (because of the very slow rate of bone growth).

Despite a wide range of clinical research, there is little evidence that taking pills and supplements can lead to safe improvement in bone structure. It is particularly noteworthy that there is a group of drugs (bisphosphonates) that do improve bone structure, but they are not proven to be safe with younger, premenopausal women, and so they should be avoided by most women with eating disorders. There is only one medicine that will safely improve bone structure in this way – food. Eating to gain weight results in the reinstatement of hormonal levels, and that is key to bone growth.

You should be aware that the evidence to date seems to suggest that even eating normally will not lead to full recovery of bone mass. However, you can regain enough bone mass to ensure that you will not have long-term problems of the sort outlined above – as long as your eating is good enough.

Fertility

Both women and men with anorexic problems experience hormonal changes that impair their libido and their fertility. The good news is that there is no evidence that those changes are permanent. In short, if your weight recovers, then you should be unaffected. Of course, this does not guarantee that you can get pregnant with ease (or at all), if you have other physical problems that would get in the way (e.g., a low natural fertility, polycystic ovaries, reached an age where getting pregnant would be difficult, being menopausal). For women, the return of their periods (often preceded by premenstrual symptoms and sexual daydreaming) is a strong indicator of a return to normal fertility levels. However, your periods do not always start at the point where fertility becomes viable. Rather like when coming off a contraceptive pill, it can take several months before your menstrual cycle returns fully. Just do not assume that you cannot get pregnant before you have had your first period, as there are cases where this has happened. Remember to use contraceptives unless you are happy to become pregnant at this point.

For female sufferers, the most effective way of finding out likely fertility levels before your periods start is to ask your doctor to arrange for a pelvic ultrasound examination (with the necessary tests for hormone levels). If you are aiming to gain weight, we usually find that there is not much point in doing this until you have reached a BMI of somewhere in the range 19–20 and held your weight stable there for several weeks (preferably while not using the contraceptive pill, as that can mask the return to biological maturity – the contraceptive pill operates by switching off your menstrual cycle). This might need to be repeated if there is no evidence of a return to fertility (particularly the return of your periods) after a further period of weight gain.

If you are bulimic, then it is strongly advisable to avoid becoming pregnant until you have stopped your bulimic behaviors. There is some evidence that such behaviors can damage the fetus in a small number of cases, but not that those effects last beyond the bulimia. The one issue that might be important to consider is that there is some overlap between bulimic disorders and polycystic ovaries – a syndrome that is associated with reduced fertility in many cases. If your periods are not regular when you are at a normal weight, then it is worth talking to your family doctor about this matter, to see if a pelvic ultrasound would indicate the need for medical treatment.

Will my eating disorder have had an impact on my children?

While many sufferers report that they are motivated to change in order to get pregnant or to be a better parent, they are often terrified that they will have done their children harm. In essence, the key issue is whether they were pregnant and/ or raised the child while they still had the eating disorder. If they did, then there is some evidence that the child's eating and psychological status can be impaired. However, if they have recovered from the eating disorder first, then there is no evidence that sufferers' children are impaired. So the best recommendation is that you work on the eating disorder first, wherever possible, before you get pregnant.

Many women "drop" their eating disorder symptoms during pregnancy (e.g., stop bingeing and vomiting). While this is undoubtedly good for the baby's development, returning to the eating disorder post-birth is likely to have an impact on your child's eating attitudes and behaviors, and on their mood. Therefore, use this time to challenge your beliefs about food, weight, and shape, in order to develop your relapse prevention skills. Similarly, if you try to lose weight rapidly post-birth, you are taking a risk that the eating disorder will recur.

Post-birth, you are likely to find what most parents do – that having a child is incompatible with your earlier levels of order and structure. Life is going to be chaos for a while, and the best you can do is to accept that fact and give yourself permission to live a life where you focus on parenthood as an achievement, rather than as a trial. This needs a lot of discussion with those around you, including some planning for how to cope with the unexpected.

19

Carers need to move on too

Having a child, partner, sister or friend with an eating disorder can be an extremely worrying and emotionally draining process. In Section 4, we discussed how much this experience can impact on the life of you and your family. If your family member or friend is moving towards recovery, you will be very pleased. However, there are some things that you might need to consider.

Understanding the sufferer's perspective

As you have read this book, you will have developed an awareness of the struggle that individuals face to recover, and of the ambivalence they feel about certain parts of their recovery (often including gaining weight). You will also have realized that recovery is a complex process, and that even though the sufferer has gained weight, stopped using behaviors, and improved physically, there can still be substantial psychological changes to make. One of the biggest fears that sufferers express is that the people around them assume they are better just because they have returned to a normal weight or stopped bingeing and purging. In fact, this is often the time when sufferers feel worst, having to face all the things that they might previously have been blocking out. Therefore, although you will be very pleased that they have gained weight and appear to be eating more normally, try to remember that this can be a very difficult time for the sufferer. Talking to him or her is usually a good idea if you want to understand their perspective.

Who is this new person?

Because the eating disorders, particularly anorexia, often start in adolescence, your loved one might have missed some elements of this developmental phase. They might need to go through some of the tasks of adolescence as part of their recovery (e.g., becoming more expressive of emotions and opinions, developing relationships, doing things on their own). Some sufferers have always presented as "good girls/boys" or "people-pleasers" as part of their illness. You will probably need to adapt to this new, autonomous, independent individual who is more willing to assert their opinions and needs. In some ways, the key task here is to negotiate the shift from a parent–child to an adult–adult relationship. This can feel stormy, but the outcome is likely to be a lot more satisfying than things staying the same.

What can I do if I think I see the eating disorder returning?

For many people with eating disorders, there is a possibility of relapse. Having seen your loved one go through their eating disorder, you are likely to be very sensitive to some of the signs that they are finding things difficult. Don't jump to conclusions straight away, but if your concern continues, you should gently broach this with the individual. If you can be honest about your concerns, it gives your loved one a chance to be open about his or her perspective. See if you can agree to monitor your concerns jointly (e.g., "We think that you might be exercising more again, but I see your point that you are just aiming to be healthy. How about if we agree just to keep an eye on it, and look out for if it seems to be getting in the way of other aspects of your life? Can we talk about it in a couple of weeks?").

However, if your loved one denies any problem, just remember that sometimes they might be correct. After having been so worried for so long, it can take a while for you to relax and feel confident that there is positive progress. There can be a period of time where you are holding your breath, waiting for disaster. Again, open discussion with your loved one is a good start to letting go of your tension.

Who was to blame for the eating disorder?

This is a common question for sufferers to ask after the eating disorder is over. The simple answer is that it is probably impossible to answer and that it might not matter anyway. The key thing at this stage is to let go of that tendency to blame yourself or the sufferer, so that you can all get on with forging new, adaptive relationships. In short, it is time for everyone to get on with their lives.

Conclusion: eating normally again

For the sufferer

In this book, we have focused on the skills you needed to help you get past your eating disorder, so that you can eat normally again and get on with living your life. According to what your eating problem was, you might have taken up to a year to reach this point in the program. Indeed, it is possible that you have had to go through this book a number of times in order to deal with your eating disorder. If it has not been as effective as you hoped, then the key question is whether you have actually done all the work that we have outlined. If there are things that you have not done (e.g., eating at a healthy level), then go back and see what else you need to do to give yourself the best chance of getting rid of your eating problems. Alternatively, it may be that it is time to consider professional help. However, if it has worked, then make sure that you keep this book somewhere safe, where you can locate it easily. That way you can remind yourself of how far you have come, and what all the hard work was about, but you can also top up the lessons that you have learned. It is time to get on with the rest of your life.

For the carer

We hope that this book has helped you to understand your loved one's eating disorder. More importantly, we hope it has been useful in guiding you as to how you could assist them to change and to eat normally again. It is important that neither you nor your loved one lets the eating disorder become a taboo topic. At the same time, it is important that the eating disorder does not govern every-body's life in the way it did in the past. While we hope that there will be no recurrence of the eating disorder, it will always be a significant part of your loved one's history (as well as your own) and to forget it now would be to forget how your loved one has had to struggle to escape their problem. Your loved one still has a lot of developing to do, and this means that you – as their carer – will also still have a lot to do. Hopefully, this time it will not be about the eating disorder but about helping them to live their life to the full.

Appendices

Appendix 1: List of self-help and support organizations

The following is only part of the enormous number of websites that offer information and access to self-help/support. We have focused on organizations that are non-profit, to ensure that you can access balanced advice locally. We have also confined ourselves to groups in English-speaking countries (though see below if you would like to recommend a similar website in another part of the world).

The Academy for Eating Disorders is based in the USA, but has an international remit. Its main web link is http://www.aedweb.org/, but they have a web link for public access to information about eating disorders: http://www.aedweb.org/eating_disorders/index.cfm.

Organizations that offer eating disorder-specific support for sufferers and carers

UK – beat (beating eating disorders) at www.b-eat.co.uk
USA – National Eating Disorders Association at www.nationaleatingdisorders.org
Canada – Anorexics and Bulimics Anonymous at http://www.anorexicsandbulimicsanonymousaba.com/index.asp
Australia – The Butterfly Foundation at http://www.thebutterflyfoundation.org.au/
New Zealand – Eating Disorders Association of New Zealand at http://www.ed.org.nz/
Please note: Website addresses can change, but these were correct at the time of going to press. While we have aimed to provide as comprehensive a list as possible, we are aware that there will be others that we have missed (particularly outside the English-speaking world). Any suggestions for additional organizations would be appreciated, particularly in countries where we have not been able to identify contacts, and we will aim to update this list in any future editions of this book.

Appendix 2: Effects of semi-starvation on behavior and physical health

Many people who restrict their intake suffer from physical, emotional, and cognitive consequences. However, they tend to attribute those problems to their eating disorder rather than to their being starved. This can lead you to feel that you are somehow damaged, and that you will never be normal. However, what a lot of people in your position do not realize is that your nutritional state contributes greatly to your problems, rather than those problems reflecting a permanent disability. We think that having this knowledge is essential in order for you to understand the nature of your eating difficulties fully and determine what to do about them.

The effects of starvation were best shown by a study from some years ago – the Minnesota study. We suggest that you read the summary in this appendix in order to consider whether some of your problems might be relieved by something as simple as eating more. Remember, this can apply whether you are underweight or not, since it is your level of food restriction (not necessarily your current weight) that can be the most important factor in determining whether you experience the symptoms described in the study.

Before you read the Minnesota study that follows, take a few minutes to think about which of the following features might apply to you. Tick them off, so that you can come back to them when your eating is better, and you can see what progress you have made.

Do you recognize any of the following features in yourself?

Attitudes and behavior related to eating
- Increased preoccupation with food
- Always planning meals
- Tendency to hoard
- Change in speed of eating
- Increased hunger

Emotional changes
- Depression
- Anxiety
- Irritability
- Apathy
- Neglected personal hygiene

Social and sexual changes
- Withdrawal
- Reduced sense of humor
- Feelings of social inadequacy
- Isolation
- Strained relationships
- Reduced sexual interest

Cognitive changes
- Impaired: concentration
- alertness
- comprehension
- judgement

Physical changes
- Gastrointestinal discomfort
- Reduced need for sleep
- Dizziness
- Headaches
- Hypersensitivity to noise and light
- Reduced strength
- Edema (swelling caused by fluid retention, usually in the feet and legs)
- Hair loss
- Reduced tolerance for cold temperatures
- Abnormal tingling/prickling sensations in hands and feet

Physical activity
- Tiredness
- Weakness
- Listlessness
- Apathy

The Minnesota Study

There is a remarkable similarity between many of the experiences seen in people who have experienced fairly long periods of semi-starvation and those seen in people with anorexia nervosa or bulimia nervosa. In the 1940s to 1950s, Ancel Keys and his team at the University of Minnesota in America studied the effects of starvation on behavior. What they found both surprised and alarmed them.

The experiment involved carefully studying 36 young, healthy, psychologically normal men, both during a period of normal eating and during a longer period of fairly severe food restriction, and after the food restriction was lifted. During the first three months of the experiment, the subjects ate normally while their behavior, personality, and eating patterns were studied in detail. Over the next six months, the men were given approximately half the amount of food that they needed to maintain their weight and they lost, on average, 25% of their original body weight. Some participants actually went down to a body mass index (BMI) of 14. Following this, there were three months of rehabilitation during which time the men were re-fed. Although the individual responses to the experiment varied greatly, the men experienced dramatic physical, psychological, and social changes as a result of the food restriction. Of note was the fact that, for many, these changes persisted even after weight returned to normal after the food restriction period.

Attitudes and behavior related to food and eating

The men's change in relationship to food was one of the most striking results of the experiment. They found it increasingly difficult to concentrate on more normal things, and became plagued by persistent thoughts of food and eating. Food became a principal topic of conversation, of reading, and of daydreams. Many men began reading cookbooks and collecting recipes, while others became interested in collecting various kitchen utensils. One man even began rummaging through rubbish bins in the hope of finding something that he might need. This desire to hoard has been seen in both people and animals that are deprived of food. Although food had been of little interest to the men prior to entering the experiment, almost 40% of them mentioned cooking as part of their post-experiment plans. Some actually did change their career to a career focused on food once the experiment was over.

The men's eating habits underwent remarkable changes during the study. Much of the day was now spent planning how they would eat their allocated food. Plus, in order to prolong their enjoyment of the food eaten, it would take them vastly longer amounts of time to eat a meal. They would eat in silence and would devote their total attention to the consumption of the food.

The subjects of the study were often caught between conflicting desires to gulp down their food ravenously and to consume it so slowly that the taste and smell of each morsel of food would be fully appreciated. By the end of the starvation period of the study, the men would dawdle for almost two hours over a meal that they previously would have consumed over a matter of minutes.

Another common behavior was that they would make unusual concoctions by mixing different foods together. Their use of salt and spices increased dramatically, and the consumption of tea and coffee increased so much that they had to be limited to nine cups per day. The use of chewing gum also became excessive and also had to be limited.

During the 12th week, the re-feeding phase of the experiment, most of these abnormal attitudes and behaviors to food persisted. Some of the men had more severe difficulties during the first six weeks of re-feeding. The free choice of ingredients stimulated "creative" and "experimental" playing with food; for example, licking off plates and very poor table manners persisted.

Binge-eating

During the restrictive phase of the experiment, all of the volunteers reported feeling more hungry. While some appeared able to tolerate this fairly well, for others it created intense concern or even became intolerable. Several of the men failed to stick to their diet and reported episodes of binge-eating followed by self-reproach. While working in a grocery store, one man:

> suffered a complete loss of willpower and ate several cookies, a sack of popcorn, and two overripe bananas before he could 'regain control' of himself. He immediately suffered a severe emotional upset, with nausea, and upon returning to the laboratory he vomited. He was self-deprecatory, expressing disgust and self criticism.

After about five months of re-feeding, the majority of the men reported some normalization of their eating patterns, but for some the difficulties in managing their food persisted. After eight months, most men had returned to normal eating patterns, although a few still had abnormal eating patterns. One man still reported consuming around 25% more than he did prior to the weight loss and "once he started to reduce but got so hungry he could not stand it."

Emotional changes

It is important to remember that the subjects were psychologically very healthy prior to the experiment but most experienced significant emotional changes as a result of semi-starvation. Many experienced periods of depression: some brief, while others experienced protracted periods of depression. Occasionally elation was observed, but this was inevitably followed by "low periods." The men's tolerance that had prior to starvation been high was replaced by irritability and frequent outbursts of anger. For most subjects, anxiety became more evident; many of the formerly even-tempered men began biting their nails or smoking if they felt nervous. Apathy was a common problem, and some men neglected various aspects of their personal hygiene. Most of the subjects experienced periods during which their emotional distress was quite severe, and all experienced the symptoms of "semi-starvation neurosis" described above.

Both observation and personality testing showed that the individual emotional response to semi-starvation varied considerably. Some of the volunteers seemed to cope very well while others displayed extraordinary disturbance following weight loss. As the emotional difficulties did not immediately reverse once food was in ready supply, it may be assumed that the abnormalities were related more to body weight than to short-term kilocalorie intake. So, we can draw the conclusion that many of the psychological disturbances seen in anorexia and bulimia nervosa can be the result of the semi-starvation process itself, and that the effects of disturbed eating patterns might need a longer time to normalize than you might have thought.

Social and sexual changes

Most of the volunteers experienced a large shift in their social behaviors. Although originally quite gregarious, the men became progressively more withdrawn and isolated. Humor and a sense of friendship and comradeship diminished markedly, amidst growing feelings of social inadequacy.

> Social initiative especially, and sociability in general, underwent a remarkable change. The men became reluctant to plan activities, to make decisions and to participate in group activities. . . they spent more and more time alone. It became 'too much trouble or too tiring' to have contact with people.

The volunteers' social contacts with women also declined sharply during semi-starvation. Those who continued to see women socially found that the relationships became strained. One man described his difficulties as follows:

> I am one of about 3 or 4 who still go out with girls. I fell in love with a girl during the control period but I see her only occasionally now. It is almost too much trouble to see her even when she visits me in the lab. It requires effort to hold her hand. Entertainment must be tame. If we see a show the most interesting part of it is contained in scenes where people are eating.

One subject graphically stated that he had "no more sexual feeling than a sick oyster." During the rehabilitation period the men's sexual interest was slow to return. Even after three months they judged themselves to be far from normal in this area. However, after eight months some or virtually all of the men had recovered their interest in sex.

Cognitive changes

The volunteers reported impaired concentration, alertness, comprehension, and judgement during semi-starvation.

Physical changes

As the six months of semi-starvation progressed, the volunteers exhibited many physical changes including the following: gastrointestinal discomfort, decreased need for sleep, dizziness, headaches, hypersensitivity to noise and light, reduced strength, edema (an excess of fluid causing swelling), hair loss, decreased tolerance of cold temperatures (cold hands and feet), and paresthesia (abnormal tingling or prickling sensations, especially in the hands and feet). There was an overall decrease in metabolism (decreased body temperature, heart rate, and respiration). As one volunteer described it, he felt as if his "body flame were burning as low as possible to conserve precious fuel and still maintain life processes."

During rehabilitation, the metabolism speeded up again, especially in those who had the larger increases in food intake. Subjects who gained the most weight described being concerned about their increased sluggishness, general flabbiness, and the tendency for the fat to accumulate around the stomach and buttocks.

These complaints are very similar to those that people with bulimia and anorexia describe as they gain weight. However, after approximately a year the men's body fat and muscle levels were back to their pre-experiment levels.

Physical activity

In general, the men responded to semi-starvation by reducing their activity levels. They became tired, weak, listless, and apathetic and complained of a lack of energy. Voluntary movements became noticeably slower. However, according to the original report,

> some men exercised deliberately at times. Some of them attempted to lose weight by driving themselves through periods of excessive energy in order to either obtain increased bread rations. . . or to avoid reduction in rations.

This is similar to the practice of many eating disorder sufferers, who feel that if they exercise strenuously they can allow themselves a bit more to eat.

Significance of the study

As all of the volunteers were psychologically and physically healthy prior to the experiment, all of the symptoms experienced by them can be put down to the period of starvation. It would appear therefore that many of the symptoms faced in anorexia nervosa and bulimia nervosa are a result of the food restriction rather than the illnesses themselves. It is important to recognize that these symptoms are not just limited to food and weight, but extend to virtually all areas of psychological and social functioning. It is therefore extremely important that a person with an eating disorder returns to a normal weight (if underweight) to allow these symptoms to reduce significantly/completely, and for both the therapist and the patient to become aware of emotional problems that underlie the eating disorder (as, unlike the men in the study, the disordered eating might have started as a way of coping with difficulties in life).

It is also important to think about how the men's relationship with food was not normal even after they returned to eating freely available food. In the short term they felt out of control with much of their food intake and were unable to identify when they felt hungry or when they felt full. Many of these symptoms continued after they reached a normal weight and, for some, took several months and years to normalize. It is therefore important for someone recovering from anorexia nervosa or bulimia nervosa to understand they cannot just expect that their body will return to being able to regulate food intake on its own. We know that consuming a well-balanced and nutritionally complete food intake, spread out over regular points during the day, minimizes the length of time that it takes for the body to recognize when it is hungry and when it is full.

Appendix 3: Complications of food restriction and low weight/anorexia nervosa

Anorexia nervosa is a potentially life-threatening condition. As well as the relatively high risk of death, it is also associated with many other serious complications. These are basically all associated with the body's attempt to conserve energy, keep warm, and find the food it needs.

The vast majority of the effects are not permanent, and are reversed once food intake and weight are normalized.

Area of the body/ system affected	Common symptoms	Why do these symptoms occur?
Gastrointestinal (gut)	• Reduced stomach size/capacity, leading to feeling full on less food than normal • Constipation • Feeling bloated • Abdominal pain	During periods of food restriction and weight loss the gut does not process food as quickly, meaning that food moves through it much more slowly. This might be because the gut muscle is too malnourished to work normally, and because the body slows processing in order to get everything it can from the food.
Fertility	• Irregular/absent menstrual periods • Reduced fertility or infertility • If pregnancy does occur the fetus is also at risk in both the short and long term if the mother does not eat enough	When food is sparse, the body reduces all processes that need large amounts of energy, such as pregnancy. The body prevents this from happening by temporarily stopping menstruation. A lack of interest in sex is also common, also reducing the likelihood of pregnancy.

Area of the body/ system affected	Common symptoms	Why do these symptoms occur?
Blood results	• Low sugar levels, leading to increased risk of bingeing, and poor concentration • Anemia • Increased risk of serious infections • Cholesterol levels increase	• A low blood sugar caused by a lack of carbohydrate sends a powerful signal to the brain to encourage the body to eat the food it needs. • Anemia can be caused by low iron intake. • White blood cell levels are the front line for protecting against infection. If food is sparse there is not enough energy or protein to make these cells. • The cause of high cholesterol is unclear, but it may be because cholesterol excretion is affected.
Tolerance to cold	• Reduced sensitivity to extremes of temperatures • Numb/cold peripheries (toes, fingers, and nose) • Hair growth on face and back (lanugo hair)	• Low body-fat levels reduce the ability to cope with extremes of temperature • Blood flow to the organs (heart, kidneys, liver, etc.) is prioritized, causing low blood flow to peripheries • Lanugo hair is one way the body has to keep warm.
Cardiovascular/ circulation	• Low blood pressure – leads to dizziness and feeling faint • Slow pulse rate • Irregular heart beat (atrial fibrillation) • Swollen feet and ankles (edema)	• The slowing down of the heart is to conserve energy. Also the heart is a muscle, so will be weakened in cases of extreme weight loss. • Edema is often an effect of suddenly stopping laxative abuse or vomiting, a sudden increase in food, or because of low body levels of protein in severe weight loss.
Bone health	• Thin bones (osteoporosis) • Not reaching optimum peak bone mass in adulthood (increasing the risk of osteoporosis in later life)	The main cause is low levels of estrogen in women (when menstrual periods stop) or low testosterone in men. This causes bones to lose strength. Peak bone mass is reached as a young adult, exactly the time most people develop anorexia. Bone health is one area where effects of anorexia can be permanent, although it can always be improved.

Area of the body/ system affected	Common symptoms	Why do these symptoms occur?
Dental health	• Gum problems – gum recession, bleeding, and weakness • Permanent erosion of teeth	• Weight loss and vitamin and mineral deficiency can cause gum disease. • High intake of acidic foods (like fruit, fizzy drinks, condiments like vinegar) can cause dental problems.
Emotional	• Irritability • Depression • Poor concentration • Feeling isolated • Fatigue and exhaustion • Anxiety • Thinking about food all the time	These responses occur for two reasons: 1. To conserve energy –we tend to do less when depressed. 2. Anxiety and thinking about food may increase the likelihood that we go out and find food to eat.
Bladder function	• Kidney infections • Poor bladder control	The kidney can become less able to concentrate urine, leading to increased urine production. Problems with the nerve supply to the bladder, and muscle loss can lead to infections.
Muscle function	• Muscle wasting and weakness	If food is very sparse the body breaks down muscle to provide energy (especially carbohydrate).
Other	• Poor sleep	Light sleep patterns are a known effect of weight loss.

Additional complications occur if low weight occurs in combination with vomiting, laxative abuse, diuretic abuse, and/or excessive exercise.

Appendix 4: Complications of bulimia nervosa (especially laxative abuse and vomiting)

Bulimia nervosa is a potentially life-threatening condition. As well as the relatively high risk of death, it is also associated with many other serious complications. These are mainly related to the effects of purging.

Area of the body/system affected	Common symptoms	Why do these symptoms occur?
Imbalance of body salts (electrolytes – sodium, potassium, and chloride)	• Irregular heart beat/ palpitations • Irregular heart beat (cardiac arrhythmia) or cardiac failure • Convulsions • Dehydration (leads to light-headedness and fainting)	Both vomiting and laxative abuse lead to large losses of body salts and water. The salts are vital in maintaining normal electrical impulses in muscle, especially the heart.
Edema (swelling) in ankles and legs	• Swollen ankles and legs	• The sudden stopping of vomiting and/or laxatives causes the body to re-hydrate (see above). • This usually resolves by day ten. • It is important to drink normally during this time (and not to restrict fluids).
Mouth/oral problems	• Swollen salivary glands (making the face look "fat") • Erosion of tooth enamel and possibly the tooth itself	• Stomach acid is vomited up into the mouth, inflaming sensitive tissues in the mouth, tongue, and throat.

Area of the body/system affected	Common symptoms	Why do these symptoms occur?
	• Frequent and widespread dental decay • Increased sensitivity to hot and cold • Sore throat/difficulty swallowing	• The acid also attacks all of the teeth, not just the few that dental decay usually affects.
Gastrointestinal (gut) – upper bowel (stomach and small intestine)	• Acid reflux • Chronic regurgitation • Esophagus and/or stomach rupture (which is usually fatal) • Bloating and abdominal pain • Distension • Bleeding in the esophagus • Pancreatitis (inflammation of the pancreas)	• Prolonged vomiting often leads to the flap of skin at the top of the stomach becoming weaker, meaning acid escapes very easily. • Bleeding is caused by the physical trauma of vomiting and needs urgent medical assessment.
Gastrointestinal (gut) – lower (large intestine)	• Damaged large bowel • Chronic constipation/impaction of feces • Piles (including bleeding) • Bowel prolapse	• Chronic use of stimulant laxatives may cause the loss of normal movement of food waste through the gut (peristalsis), leading to constipation, and possibly piles. • Prolapse can occur because of weakness of the pelvic floor.
Eyes/face	• Eyes can be bloodshot • Small red spots can occur on the face	• The strain of vomiting causes bleeding in the eyes and facial skin, which resolve once vomiting stops.
Kidney and bladder infections	• Pain on passing urine • Pus/blood in urine	• Dehydration increases the risk of infection. • Fecal contamination of urinary tract (common with diarrhea)
Lungs	• Lung infections/pneumonia	• Vomit can pass into the lungs. • The acid will burn the lungs. • Bacteria can cause an infection.

N.B. If you vomit, AVOID brushing your teeth immediately after vomiting. This is because it brushes acid into the teeth throughout your mouth, increasing the risk of dental problems. Instead, rinse your mouth out (including under the tongue) with water or fluoridated mouthwash.

Additional complications commonly seen in anorexia nervosa will probably also be experienced, especially if you are at a relatively low weight, have recently lost a lot of weight, or are following a very restrictive diet.

Appendix 5: The effect of self-induced vomiting on physical health

You may make yourself sick after eating or bingeing in the hope that it will help you control your food intake and your weight. While on the surface it seems a perfect way of eating freely without gaining weight (although it is important to be aware that this is far from true since around 1200 kilocalories are retained if vomiting occurs after a binge), there are many health risks involved with this behavior.

Electrolyte (body salts) imbalance

When you vomit you will not only get rid of some of the food you have eaten, but also many essential salts (potassium, sodium, and chloride) that keep nerve and muscle function normal. This leads to:
- Irregular heart beat/palpitations
- Fatigue
- Muscle weakness and spasms (made worse by over-exercise)
- Irritability
- Convulsions
- Cardiac failure

Dehydration

Consistently making yourself sick will lead to dehydration. The effects of chronic dehydration are:
- Feeling thirsty all the time
- Light-headedness
- Feeling weak
- Fainting (especially on standing)
- Frequent urinary tract infections (e.g., cystitis)
- Kidney damage

Drinking excessive amounts of water will not reduce the dehydration, and may make it worse. This is owing to the fact that the essential salts are needed to allow the body to absorb the fluid.

When you stop vomiting there will probably be a temporary weight gain owing to rehydration. This can show itself as puffy fingers, but also slight swelling in the ankles and feet. This can cause much alarm, but in fact is only of medical concern if the swelling extends above the knee. At this point it is important to seek medical advice. Otherwise, rest and raise the feet whenever possible and it will resolve in a few days. Diuretics are not necessary, except in severe cases, when your doctor may prescribe them for a short time. Avoid self-medicating with diuretics.

Problems with teeth

Vomiting for more than a few months is likely to cause dental problems. The important thing to note is that, unlike ordinary dental decay, the damage is likely to affect all of your teeth, and can require very extensive dental treatment. In order to limit the problems, it is important to avoid brushing your teeth for at least an hour after vomiting. The main dental problems seen in chronic vomiting are:
- Erosion of tooth enamel
- Frequent cavities
- Sensitivity to hot and cold food and drinks
- An unsightly smile!

Stomach problems

Chronic vomiting can cause problems throughout the whole of your gut:
- Swollen salivary glands (leading to a swollen "chipmunk" face)
- Sore tongue, mouth, and throat, which can lead to a hoarse voice
- Inflamed/bleeding esophagus (also known as the windpipe or gullet)
- Distension of the stomach and esophagus (ruptures can occur, which can have fatal consequences)

Problems with eyes

Vomiting can cause eyes to become bloodshot, which while harmless, is unsightly.

Other problems

It is possible for vomit to pass into the lungs, which may cause lung infections and pneumonia.

Appendix 6: The effects of laxative abuse on physical health

Laxatives are medications used on a short-term basis to relieve constipation. There are several different types, which have different roles depending on the cause of the constipation. Some are available over the counter from pharmacists, while others are only available on prescription. Many over-the-counter laxatives are described as "natural" or "herbal," which suggests they are safe, and carry no risk. However, this is not the case. The most common type of laxative abused in eating disorders are stimulant laxatives, such as Senokot or Dulcolax. (N.B. Laxatives prescribed under medical supervision are fine, especially since the doctor will usually prescribe a different type of laxative – usually one that is bulk-forming, such as Fybogel or Lactulose).

You may have started to take laxatives because of a belief that they will help you lose weight, or to compensate for eating more food than you feel comfortable with. Abuse of stimulant laxatives will leave you feeling empty, with a much-desired flat stomach, and convinced that you have not gained weight. However, any weight loss and change in body shape is the result of the dehydrating effect of watery diarrhea and the complete emptying of the large bowel. It is nothing to do with changes in fat, muscle or carbohydrate levels in the body. This is because laxatives work on the large intestine, whereas food is digested and absorbed in the small intestine.

Laxative abuse can have serious side effects on health, many related to low potassium levels (hypokalemia) secondary to watery diarrhea. This can be severe enough to trigger dangerous cardiac problems and other medical problems, while the long-term dehydration related to laxative abuse can lead to kidney failure or problems with kidney function. Other problems that can occur include rectal bleeding (probably related to chemical irritation from the laxatives), urinary tract infections, muscle weakness, confusion or convulsions.

Laxative abuse may also cause you problems when you try to stop taking them. The large bowel gets tolerant to the levels of laxatives taken, so you may have found you needed to take more and more to get the same effect. Stopping them suddenly is then likely to cause water retention (as the body gets used to not having to retain every drop of water to minimize dehydration). It is possible for weight to increase up to 5 kg or more when laxatives are stopped abruptly, owing to the fluid levels returning to normal. The rise in weight is detectable both from the weighing scales (which can reinforce the belief that laxatives lead to weight control), and from seeing differences in your body, such as feeling more bloated, plus possible temporary swelling of the feet and ankles. This swelling is called rebound edema and usually lasts for 10–14 days after stopping laxative abuse, following which weight drops slightly owing to normalization of body water levels.

You may also experience constipation when you stop taking laxatives. However, there are healthy ways to help your body return to normal bowel function, such as making sure you eat a range of foods that contain dietary fiber (wholemeal or granary bread, high fiber breakfast cereals, brown rice, lentils and beans (e.g., kidney beans), and fruit and vegetables), drinking enough fluids (around 1.5–2 litres a day) and developing a routine for going to the toilet (even if you don't find it easy to pass a bowel motion to start with). Giving up laxatives can be really anxiety-provoking so talk to your carer if you feel you need more support. Your family doctor could also be a useful ally – take this information sheet and a record of how many laxatives you take with you to help him/her understand your difficulties.

Appendix 7: The effects of diuretic abuse on physical health

People with eating disorders sometimes take diuretics (also known as water tablets) because they believe that the weight lost is caused by loss of fat. In fact, diuretics have no effect whatsoever on kilocalorie absorption, and the weight loss seen is caused by water loss. As soon as the diuretics are stopped, rehydration occurs, and weight returns to normal.

Non-prescription (over-the-counter) diuretics

While over-the-counter diuretics rarely cause medical problems, they can contain very high levels of caffeine. This can lead to headaches, trembling, and a rapid heart rate. Caffeine can also greatly increase anxiety.

Prescription diuretics

Abuse of prescription diuretics tends to be more dangerous.

Dehydration

Consistent abuse of diuretics will lead to dehydration, the chronic effects of which are:
• Feeling thirsty all the time
• Light-headedness
• Feeling weak
• Fainting (especially on standing)
• Frequent urinary tract infections (e.g., cystitis)
• Kidney damage

Electrolyte (body salts) imbalance

When you abuse diuretics you will get rid of many essential salts (potassium, sodium, and chloride) that keep nerve and muscle function normal. This leads to:
• Irregular heart beat/palpitations
• Weakness
• Muscle weakness and spasms (made worse by over-exercise)
• Irritability
• Convulsions
• Cardiac failure
N.B. These effects are likely to be worse if you also abuse laxatives and/or regularly vomit.

Low levels of magnesium in the blood

This is called hypomagnesemia. It can make the symptoms of low potassium worse, and can result in arrhythmias (abnormal heart rhythms) and even in sudden death.

Urine problems

Abuse of tablets that stimulate urine production will potentially cause problems with passing urine:
• Polyuria (producing large amounts of urine)
• Blood in urine (hematuria)
• Pyuria (pus in urine)

Kidney damage

Long-term abuse of diuretics can eventually lead to kidney problems owing to the effect of chronic dehydration, and also owing to the toxic effect of the diuretics on the kidneys.

Other problems

Diuretics can cause several other problems, such as:
• Nausea
• Abdominal pain
• Constipation

Appendix 8: Exercise and activity

We frequently hear about the need to be more active to improve our chances of remaining healthy. Most of the general population need to increase their activity in order to improve their long-term health. However, many people with eating disorders go too far the other way and are too active, which can also have severe health consequences.

"Excessive" versus "compulsive" exercise

The diagnostic criteria for eating disorders often include the fact the person uses "excessive" levels of exercise. However, it is difficult to define this objectively, and it is now recognized that it is more relevant to consider whether the person feels a *compulsion* to exercise. Therefore, it is important to think both about how much activity you do, and also about *why* you are active.

Common difficulties with activity levels seen in people with an eating disorder include:

Excessive activity

Although it is difficult to define this objectively, doing more than four hours of activity or exercise per week is probably an excessive level, unless you are a competitive athlete. Activity could be anything such as walking, running, exercise classes, extreme forms of yoga, and very high levels of housework.

Compulsive activity

The person has a belief that they must do an exact number of repetitions (e.g., exactly 300 sit-ups) of an exercise, or something bad will happen.

Both excessive and compulsive levels of activity are unhealthy and possibly dangerous, so therefore need to be addressed in eating disorder treatment.

How much activity is healthy?

The Department of Health recommends the following as a minimum for the general population:

How much?	30 minutes a day.
How often?	At least 5 days of the week.
How intense?	Moderate – the person should be warm and slightly out of breath during activity, but still be able to hold a conversation. This level will be different for everybody.
What counts?	Activity can be regular, organized exercise (e.g., a tennis class, aerobics) but also includes activities of daily living (e.g., walking to the bus stop, housework).
The motivation?	The healthiest reason people exercise is because they enjoy it. They may want to improve their physical health, including toning up, or perhaps even losing a little weight, but this is not the primary motivation to exercise.

Risks of excessive exercise

Although the 30 minutes, five days a week is a minimum, there are implications of being *too* active. Excessive exercise can:
- Increase the risk of injury and even permanent damage.
- Lead to dehydration/fluid balance fluctuations (especially if the person is also purging).
- Lead to exhaustion and impaired performance.
- Result in poor concentration.
- Lead to weight loss (owing to energy expenditure) or weight gain (through building muscle), and a change in body shape.
- Lead to infrequent or absent menstrual periods, increasing the risk of osteoporosis.

Appendix 9: The effect of purging on calorie absorption

Many people with eating disorders eat more than they feel comfortable with, either regularly or occasionally. This can lead to many emotions like panic, anger, guilt, and shame, and often results in methods to try and rid the body of the excess kilocalories eaten, thus regaining control – but how effective are these behaviors?

Self-induced vomiting

"How many kilocalories are lost?"
- Researchers have found that on average around 1200 kilocalories are retained after self-induced vomiting, whether the binge was relatively small (around 1500 kilocalories) or relatively large (around 3500 kilocalories) (Kaye *et al.*, 1993).
- "Markers" used to judge when all the food has been purged (e.g., eating carrots first so that the orange colour in vomit indicates complete gastric emptying) are ineffective because of the fact that the stomach mixes food up during and after the eating process.
- Many people who binge and purge report that they gain weight over time, which suggests that the body learns how to retain kilocalories, despite vomiting.

"But vomiting helps me gain control – doesn't it?"
- After eating, the body produces insulin to mop up the sugar it expects to absorb from the food. Purging gets rid of some of this food but the insulin levels remain as high, resulting in a low blood sugar around an hour or two later. A low blood sugar level sends a strong signal to the brain saying, "I AM HUNGRY – FEED ME!" resulting in a strong urge to binge again.
  - Therefore, instead of purging because you have binged, you are possibly bingeing because you have purged.

- Many people say that once they have decided to purge, they eat more as they expect to get rid of all the food through purging. Since around the equivalent of two normal-sized meals are retained regardless of the size of the binge, it could be argued that you are more in control if you eat a normal meal and avoid vomiting afterwards.

Laxative abuse

"How many kilocalories are lost?"
- Laxatives work on the large bowel, whereas kilocalories are absorbed in the upper, small bowel. So it is no surprise that Bo-Linn and colleagues (1983) found that laxatives decrease kilocalorie absorption by at most 12% each time they are used, despite 4–6 litres of diarrhea.

"But laxatives help me gain control – don't they?"
- After laxatives, the empty feeling and flat stomach probably feel very good. However, as soon as you start eating again the effects are lost, and many people feel more full and bloated than if they avoided the laxatives in the first place.
- Long-term abuse of laxatives can result in constipation and bloating when you stop taking them because the bowel has become "lazy" since it has relied on the laxatives for so long.

Diuretics/water tablets

"How many kilocalories are lost?"
- Diuretics have no effect on kilocalorie absorption. Weight loss after taking water tablets results from fluid losses only, and will be regained once the effects of the water tablets have worn off, and fluids are drunk.

Appendix 10: Weight control in the short and long term

Weight is a major concern for people with an eating disorder. A strong desire to control body weight often leads to restrictive eating, vomiting, and other purging methods.

It is important to understand how the body regulates weight in both the short and long term, and to learn how to recognize the difference between the two.

Short-term weight changes

- This means the alterations seen on a daily basis.
- It relates to the type of food eaten, hormonal changes, and changes related to fluid balance over the course of the day, and does not indicate that you have become fat overnight.
- Some women find that they gain weight just before their period, regardless of whether they are on the Pill or not, and that they return to the old weight a day or so after the period starts.
- We all will see an increase in weight from the beginning of the day to the end based on the fact that we retain 2–3 lb (1–1.5 kg) of fluid over the course of the day, which gets excreted as urine after laying down overnight.

Long-term weight changes

- This means changes to fat and/or muscle stores.
- It is related to your energy intake over weeks and months, not days.
- If you eat what your body needs in terms of energy over several weeks your weight will remain stable.
- If you eat less than your body needs over several weeks you will lose weight.
- If you eat more than your body needs over several weeks you will gain weight.

How do long-term and short-term weight relate?

- In order to be able to see the long-term weight changes (i.e., changes to body fat and muscle content) we need to look beyond the day-to-day fluctuations in our weight.
- Weighing yourself once a week is sufficient to see long-term weight patterns – weighing yourself more frequently than this will probably result in huge anxiety because of the daily weight fluctuations related to changes in body fluid levels.
- Eating disorder behaviors such as purging (vomiting or abusing laxatives), and bingeing/overeating after a period of restriction all lead to fluid loss (dehydration) and then short-term water retention when the behaviors stop. This makes it much more difficult to assess what is really happening with the weight.
- At least four weighings over several weeks are needed to identify trends in "real" weight (i.e., those related to fat and muscle changes).

Appendix 11: The advantages of regular eating

To recover fully from an eating disorder you will need to learn to use food to meet your physical needs rather than as a way of coping with emotional difficulties. This involves eating three balanced meals with two to three planned, appropriate snacks each day. The healthy eating plan outlined in this book (Chapter 9, Step 2) will give you that structure.

Developing a regular, balanced pattern of eating

Eating three meals and regular snacks each day is helpful for the following reasons:
- You don't have to face very large meals.
- The gaps between meals are more manageable.
- It helps avoid the feeling that you may lose control of what you are eating.
- It helps ensure you get the full range of nutrients that you need, as you will naturally tend to eat a wider variety of foods.

Hunger

People with eating problems often feel they cannot tell when they are physically hungry or physically full. Reasons for this include:
- Current or previous weight loss seems to alter the body's ability to recognize hunger and fullness, even after a normal body weight is achieved. This is temporary but may take several months, if not longer to return to normal.
- How you feel may have a direct effect on hunger and satiety (fullness). For example, when you are anxious, you might feel either more or less hungry than when you are not anxious.

A regular, balanced type of meal plan is more physically satisfying, which helps your body regulate feelings of hunger and fullness to enable them to return to being natural reflexes.

Overeating/bingeing

- Since you are meeting your body's physical needs, you are less likely to overeat because of hunger.
- If you are not chronically hungry, you are more likely to be able to reflect on how to handle a situation, rather than reaching for food as your first response to a problem.

Weight/physical issues

- Whether you are at a normal weight or working to gain weight, following an eating plan will minimize short-term weight fluctuations related to body fluid shifts, thus making weight changes more predictable.
- Eating infrequently can lead to an increase in body fat. This is partly because your metabolism slows down slightly, and partly because when you do eat, you are more likely to overeat, meaning that the excess will probably be stored as fat.
- Eating regularly (including breakfast) is the most effective method of maintaining a healthy weight over a long period of time.
- A balanced food intake increases the likelihood that your periods will return at a lower rather than a higher weight.

Metabolic rate (how quickly you use up energy)

- Chronic undereating can cause weight gain by lowering your metabolic rate (see the point under Weight/physical issues, above).
- Regular eating normalizes your metabolic rate, minimizing physical problems such as feeling cold all the time and feeling moody/irritable.

Concentration and ability to do academic work

- After a short time of eating regularly you will spend less time thinking about food, bingeing or purging, meaning you have more space to do academic work (e.g., college work, paid work).
- Skipping meals, especially breakfast, can reduce your ability to solve problems rationally, and reduce your academic performance.

Appendix 12: General points to help normalize your food intake

When you start to change your eating habits, it can be confusing to work out what to do. These points give you some basic tips to help, and offer some explanation as to why they are important.

1. Leave no more than 3–4 hours between meals and snacks. This relates to blood sugar control, which is a key player in appetite control. After 3–4 hours your blood sugar will start to drop, as the energy from the last meal or snack has been used up. This drop in blood sugar sends a strong signal to the brain that you need to eat something. If you leave it for longer than this you may find yourself craving sugary and fatty foods, increasing the risk of overeating.

2. Do not rely on hunger to tell you when to eat – eating disorders often cause hunger perceptions to become distorted and unreliable.

3. Make it a priority to eat regularly – aim not to skip meals or snacks as this is likely to increase physical cravings for food later on (see point 1, above), and most people find it extremely hard to reintroduce food once it has been cut out.

In the beginning, this pattern may feel like you are eating all the time, but after a while this pattern helps you worry less about eating, since cravings for food will diminish.

4. Once you have started following the basic meal plan of three meals and two to three snacks, try not to eat more than this, as your body has all it needs from your eating plan.

   • If you cannot stop yourself from eating between planned meals and snacks, get back on track with your eating plan as soon as possible. Don't miss your next meal/snack to compensate – after all, the extra that you have eaten is unlikely to affect your weight dramatically, whereas missing meals/snacks is likely to lead to further uncontrolled eating, which is likely to affect your weight.

5. Be realistic about goals around eating – think about easiest changes first and build up to more challenging ones later, when you feel more confident. Introduce change gradually. Think about your typical day, when you are least chaotic or feel more secure about your eating pattern, and start there.

Appendix 13: Healthy eating

These points come from the book *Eating Disorders: The Facts* (Abraham and Llewellyn-Jones, 1992). They do not represent an agreed definition about what constitutes healthy eating, but are more the opinion of that book's authors. Therefore, it may be useful to go through these points, decide whether you agree with them and, if not, think about how you would define healthy eating.

Healthy eating *IS*:
- eating something at least three times a day
- eating more than you feel you need to eat on some occasions (overeating)
- eating less than you need on other occasions (undereating)
- eating more of the foods that you enjoy the taste of, when you choose to
- eating less of the foods you like, as you know you can eat them in the future
- eating or not eating on occasions because you feel unhappy, "bad", or tense
- eating both "good" and "bad" foods, in other words a variety of foods, without feeling guilty
- eating in a flexible way so that it does not interfere with your work, study or social life
- eating sufficient food and a variety of foods, often enough to prevent a desire to binge-eat
- eating, when out socially, in a similar manner to the other people in the group
- eating at "fast food" outlets occasionally, as a treat to yourself
- being aware that eating is not the most important thing in life, but knowing that it is important for good health

Healthy eating is *NOT*:
- counting kilocalories, weighing food, or following a strict diet
- always eating low kilocalorie foods – for example, diet biscuits rather than bread
- eating to lose weight
- assuming that you can control the amount and type of food your body needs better than your body can

- having to constantly weigh yourself for reassurance
- playing games with yourself to prevent eating certain foods that you like – for example, by saying to yourself "dairy products make me feel nauseous" or "I've become vegan for health reasons" when the real reason is to justify excessive amounts of fruit and vegetables

Appendix 14: Examples of different foods and the food group that they belong to

	Bread, other cereals, and potatoes	Meat, fish, and alternatives	Milk and dairy foods	Fruit and vegetables	Fats important for health	Foods that have fat/sugar
What food is included?	Bread, crackers, pasta, cous cous, rice, potatoes, breakfast cereals, cracked wheat, (bulgar), oats, plain biscuits (e.g., Digestives)	Meat, fish (white & oily), poultry, meat products (e.g., sausages), fish products (e.g., fish fingers), eggs, lentils & pulses (e.g., kidney beans, baked beans), vegetarian products (e.g., quorn, tofu), nuts & seeds	Milk, cheese, yoghurt, fromage frais, calcium-enriched soya products	Fresh, frozen & canned fruit & vegetables, & dried fruit (a glass of fruit juice counts once per day)	Margarine, butter, oils, oily salad dressings (mainly from polyunsaturated or monounsaturated sources, not saturated)	Chocolate, crisps, sweets, pastries, cakes, rich puddings, sugar added to foods
Main nutrients they provide	Carbohydrate, (starch), dietary fiber, some calcium & iron B vitamins	Protein, iron, B vitamins, especially B12, zinc, magnesium	Calcium, protein vitamin B12, vitamin A & D	Vitamin C, carotenes, (a form of vitamin A), folate, dietary fiber, some carbohydrate	Fats, vitamin D, E & K, essential fatty acids	Mainly provide fat & sugar, but many contain other nutrients

(cont.)

	Bread, other cereals, and potatoes	Meat, fish, and alternatives	Milk and dairy foods	Fruit and vegetables	Fats important for health	Foods that have fat/sugar
How much to choose	Should be eaten every 3–4 hours. Include a good portion at each meal, plus at some snacks	Most people need 2 portions per day, although some need three	Most people need three portions per day	Five portions per day	Small portion (such as 2–3 teaspoons) at most meals, but especially lunch and dinner	Most "normal eaters" consume between 1–3 portions per day

Appendix 15: Carbohydrates: some basic facts

Summary of functions of carbohydrates in the body

- Provides the body's preferred source of energy. It can use other energy sources (e.g., fat, protein and alcohol, but does not work as well on them in either the short or the long term)
- Provides energy for the brain and central nervous system
- Regulates blood sugar levels
- Prevents the use of protein to meet energy needs
- Prevents the formation of dangerous by-products (ketones) when fat is burned for energy
- Provides dietary fiber to protect against heart disease and cancer
- Contributes to feelings of fullness
- Provides fiber to prevent constipation

How much energy does carbohydrate provide?

- 1g of carbohydrate provides 3.75 kilocalories.
- An average portion of carbohydrate food (e.g., two slices of bread) contains around 30–35g of carbohydrate.

How much carbohydrate do we need?

- Carbohydrate should be around half of the total energy we eat each day. For the average female who needs around 2000 kcalories a day, this works out to be around 250–300g of carbohydrate.
- The majority of this should be from starchy carbohydrates, milk and dairy products (which contain lactose, or "milk sugar"), and natural sugars (e.g., in

fruit). This means that each main meal and many snacks should be based on starchy carbohydrates (e.g., rice, pasta, breakfast cereal).

- Healthy eating guidelines also allow the consumption of small amounts of foods with added sugars (e.g., chocolate, cakes), and foods that are naturally high in sugar (e.g., fruit juice or honey). Generally, these kinds of foods (and other treat foods like crisps) can be eaten 1–3 times a day.

Appendix 16: Fats: some basic facts

Summary of functions of fats in the body

- Body fat keeps us warm.
- It protects internal organs (e.g., kidneys) from impact, like falls or knocks.
- Dietary fat provides the essential fatty acids linolenic acid and linoleic acid (also known as omega 3 and omega 6 fatty acids). We need to eat these on a daily basis because:
  - they are also very important in optimizing brain function (e.g., when returning to a normal weight after being a low weight; for the brain development of unborn babies).
  - they also have a role in preventing heart disease.
- Fats provide the fat-soluble vitamins A, D, E and K, all of which are essential.
- Fats contribute to the structure of blood vessels, and form a major component of the cell wall. A low fat intake will therefore increase the risk of bruising very easily, and affect skin health.
- Fats transport cholesterol around the body. Many people who are a low weight can have a high cholesterol level, which reduces if fat is added to the diet and weight is gained.
- Fat contributes to the structure of hormones, such as estrogen. A lack of estrogen will lead to a lack of periods, which increases the risk of osteoporosis. Therefore, a diet low in fat may delay the return of menstruation, or the body may need to be a higher weight before periods return, if a low-fat diet is consumed.
- Fats provide a concentrated form of energy, and act as an emergency source of energy when food is not available.
- Dietary fat helps increase feelings of fullness, therefore reducing the risk of bingeing.
- Fat gives taste and aroma to food, as well as making it tender.

How much energy does fat provide?

- 1g of fat provides 9 kilocalories.
- An average portion of fat food (e.g., the margarine on two slices of bread) contains around 10 g of fat.

How much fat do we need?

- Women need to consume between 65–77 g of fat per day, whereas men need to have between 83–97 g of fat a day to meet basic requirements.
- Around half of dietary fat should come from foods naturally high in fat (e.g., cheese, oily fish, meat, nuts, seeds etc.), and the rest should come from fats added to foods or used in cooking (e.g., oils, butter, margarine).

What are healthy levels of fat in the body and in the diet?

- A healthy fat level is approximately 20–25% of body weight for females and 10–15% for males.
- Levels lower than this are likely to lead to reduced resistance to disease, weakness, irritability, increased risk of bingeing, and reduced fertility.

Appendix 17: Diary sheet

Food and drink diary (record of everything that you eat and drink across 24 hours)

Day: _____

Date: _____

Time	Food and liquids consumed - type and amount - including alcohol	*Objective binge?	*Subjective binge?	Vomit (V) / Laxatives(L)	Context (Where was I? Who was about? What was I doing? Emotional state?)

***Objective binge** = feeling out of control, and eating a very large amount of food.
***Subjective binge** = feeling out of control, but only eating a small or normal amount.

Appendix 18: Thought record sheet

Every time I find myself (INSERT ACTION HERE)................................
....

Date/Time	What did I do?	What was going on at the time (context)?	What was I feeling that made me act that way?	What thoughts was I having that made me feel and act that way?	What alternative way of thinking about that situation might have been more helpful?	What might have been a better way of dealing with that situation?

Appendix 19: Planning a behavioral experiment

Belief to be tested	Behavioral experiment	Prediction	Alternative prediction	Outcome	Re-rate cognition	Plan
(Rate belief 0%–100%)	What will I do to test the belief? When will I do it? (Rate belief 0%–100%)	What exactly do I think will happen? How will I know whether it has happened or not?	What else might happen? (Rate belief 0%–100%)	What actually happened? Was the original prediction correct?	On balance, what is my view now? How do I rate the original beliefs in the light of the experiment?	What can I do now to further test the belief?

Appendix 20: Your therapy blueprint

My therapy blueprint

Identify your previous pattern of thoughts, feelings, behaviors, and physical state:

Write down an account of how you developed your eating disorder, and what kept it going for so long:

Identify risk factors and risky situations that might prompt you to return to your eating disorder:

Write an account of what your CBT has done to help you (i.e., what alternative strategies has CBT taught you for coping?):

References and further reading

References cited in this book

Abraham, S., & Llewellyn-Jones, D. (1992). *Eating Disorders: The Facts, 3rd edition.* Oxford: Oxford University Press.

Bo-Linn, G. W., Santa Ana, C. A., Morawski, S. G., & Fordtran, J. S. (1983). Purging and calorie absorption in bulimic patients and normal women. *Annals of Internal. Medicine,* **99**, 14–17.

Fairburn, C. G., & Harrison, P. J. (2003). Eating disorders. *Lancet,* **361**, 407–416.

Garner, D. M., & Garfinkel, P. E. (1997). *Handbook of Treatment for Eating Disorders, 2nd edition.* New York, NY: Guilford.

Gauntlett-Gilbert, J., & Grace, C. (2005). *Overcoming Weight Problems.* London: Robinson.

Highet, N., Thompson, M., & King, R. M. (2005). The experience of living with a person with an eating disorder. *Eating Disorders: The Journal of Treatment and Prevention,* **13**, 327–344.

Kaye, W. H., Weltzin, T. E., Hsu, L. K., McConaha, C. W., & Bolton, B. (1993). Amount of calories retained after binge eating and vomiting. *American Journal of Psychiatry,* **150**, 969–971.

Keys, A., Brozek, J., Henschel, A., Mickelsen, O., & Taylor, H. L. (1950). *The Biology of Human Starvation.* Minnesota, MN: University of Minnesota Press.

National Institute for Health and Clinical Excellence (2004). Eating disorders: core interventions in the treatment and management of anorexia nervosa, bulimia nervosa and related eating disorders. *Clinical Guideline 9.* London, UK: National Collaborating Centre for Mental Health.

Treasure, J., Murphy, T., Szmukler, G., *et al.* (2001). The experience of caregiving for severe mental illness: a comparison between anorexia nervosa and psychosis. *Social Psychiatry and Psychiatric Epidemiology,* **36**, 343–347.

Treasure, J., & Schmidt, U. (2008). Motivational interviewing in eating disorders. In *Motivational Interviewing and the Promotion of Mental Health,* ed. Arkowitz, H.,Westra, H., Miller, W. R., & Rollnick, S. New York, NY: Guilford Press, pp. 194–224.

Treasure, J., Smith, G., & Crane, A. (2007). *Skills-based Learning for Caring for a Loved One with an Eating Disorder: The New Maudsley Method.* London: Routledge.

Waller, G., Cordery, H., Corstorphine, E., *et al.* (2007). *Cognitive Behavioral Therapy for the Eating Disorders: A Comprehensive Treatment Guide.* Cambridge: Cambridge University Press.

Further reading: other self-help books that you might find useful for additional problems

There are many self-help books on the market, covering a wide range of problems. We have chosen ones that we and our patients with eating disorders have found most readable and helpful. If you want to know what other sufferers feel about the accessibility and usefulness of these books, then we suggest that you look on Amazon.com (or your local site) and read the reviews that other users have posted:

Burns, D. D. (2000). *Feeling Good: The New Mood Therapy.* New York, NY: Avon.

Butler, G. (2009). *Overcoming Social Anxiety and Shyness.* London: Robinson.

Fennell, M. (2009). *Overcoming Low Self-Esteem.* London: Robinson.

Gilbert, P. (2009). *Overcoming Depression.* London: Robinson.

Kennerley, H. (2000). *Overcoming Childhood Trauma.* London: Robinson.

Kennerley, H. (2009). *Overcoming Anxiety.* London: Robinson.

Ogden, J. (1992). *Fat Chance! The Myth of Dieting Explained.* London: Routledge.

Padesky, C. A., & Greenberger, D. (1995). *Mind over Mood: Change How You Feel by Changing the Way You Think.* New York, NY: Guilford.

Veale, D., & Wilson, R. (2009). *Overcoming Obsessive-Compulsive Disorder.* London: Robinson.

Young, J. E., & Klosko, J. S. (1993). *Reinventing Your Life.* New York, NY: Plume Publishers.

Index

Locators for headings which also have subheadings refer to general aspects of the topic only
Locators in *italic* refer to figures/diagrams